Cakes and Cake Decorating

CAKES
& CAKE
DECORATING

Zoe Leigh

OCTOPUS

page 1 : Soldier Birthday Cake
pages 2–3 : Devil's Food Cake

First published 1974 by Octopus Books Limited
59 Grosvenor Street, London W1

© 1974 Octopus Books Limited

ISBN 0 7064 0286 3

Produced by Mandarin Publishers Limited
Westlands Road, Quarry Bay, Hong Kong
and printed in Hong Kong

Contents

Cakes

Cake-making is one of life's more pleasurable occupations simply because it does not fall into the category of routine cooking. Basic meals have to be provided, day after day, with monotonous regularity, but cakes are something different, something special, and something apart. One usually makes them because one wants to and not because one *has* to and for this very reason one's approach is tempered with enthusiasm and eagerness rather than with boredom and marginal irritation at having to produce something for supper yet again!

I am often asked if there is any magical formula for making THE perfect cake and my answer is always 'No'. A sound recipe, carefully followed; an oven that is in good working order; the right tools for the job; all these contribute to success and if what you have baked looks good and tastes good, what more could you – or indeed anyone else – ask?

I have attempted, in this book, to cover as much ground as possible, but obviously there are omissions. This is inevitable. What I do earnestly hope is that amid the miscellany of assorted recipes there is something for everyone, be it a simple family cake for a children's tuck-in or an exotic gateau for a very special and important occasion.

Zoe Leigh

Bournvita loaf; Ginger shorties; Afternoon tea ring; Chocolate cake surprise

Weights and Measures

All measurements in this book are based on Imperial weights and measures, with American equivalents given in parenthesis.
Measurements in weight in the Imperial and American systems are the same.
Measurements in volume are different:

Spoon Measurements

Imperial	**US**
1 teaspoon (5 ml.)	1 teaspoon
1 tablespoon (20 ml.)	$1\frac{1}{4}$ tablespoons (abbrev.: T)

Liquid Measurements

1 Imperial pint	20 fl. oz.
1 American pint	16 fl. oz.
1 American cup	8 fl. oz.

Metric Measures

1 litre	$1\frac{3}{4}$ pints (working equivalent)
$\frac{1}{2}$ litre	1 pint (working equivalent)
$\frac{1}{2}$ kilogramme (500 grammes)	1 lb. (working equivalent)

All oven temperatures are given in °F, followed by the equivalent Gas Mark.

Oven Description	Setting	Gas
Very cool	250°F (121°C)	$\frac{1}{4}$
	275°F (135°C)	$\frac{1}{2}$
Cool	300°F (149°C)	1, 2
Warm	325°F (163°C)	3
Moderate	350°F (177°C)	4
Moderately hot	375°F (191°C)	5
	400°F (204°C)	6
Hot	425°F (218°C)	7
Very Hot	450°F (232°C)	8
	475°F (246°C)	9

Exmoor honey tarts

Simple cakes

These are the plain members of the cake family, mainly because they are non-rich and simple. They are the sort of cut-and-come-again efforts that constitute the ideal family cake. Quick, reasonably economical and easy for the housewife to prepare and bake, they are enthusiastically greeted by children – who, in the main, prefer the plain to the fancy – by guests at morning coffee parties or afternoon get-togethers, and by sweet-toothed husbands who sometimes tend to find the more elaborate cakes and gateaux rather rich for everyday eating. More of this style of cake – from curranty rock buns and refrigerator cookies to wedges of moist date and walnut and crumbly shortbread – have found their way into lunch boxes than any other. Their popularity is well justified, for rubbed-in cakes and cookies are tender, flavourful, temptingly golden-crusted and wholesome and, provided the recipe is accurately followed, stable and not nearly as temperamental as some of their richer relations! The usual proportions for rubbed-in cakes are half – or sometimes a little under half – fat and sugar to flour: 3–4 oz. (6–8 T) fat and sugar to 8 oz. (2 cups) unsifted self-raising or plain (all-purpose) flour. If the plain flour is used, 3 level teaspoons baking powder should be allowed for every 8 oz. (2 cups). Innumerable additions may be tossed with the dry ingredients – such as dried fruits, chopped nuts, grated lemon or orange peel, mixed chopped peel, etc. – and the flour may be sifted with spices such as cinnamon, ginger, nutmeg, etc. for flavour variations. For chocolate flavoured cakes, some of the flour may be replaced by cocoa powder and, for a deeper colour, soft brown sugar substituted for castor (granulated). The usual liquids used to bind together the ingredients are eggs plus milk or a combination of milk and fruit juice.

For success, all ingredients to be used should be at kitchen temperature and not taken straight from the refrigerator. The flour, salt and spices should be lightly sifted into a large mixing bowl. The fat should then be cut into the flour mixture with a pastry-cutter or round-topped knife until it is in small pieces and then rubbed in with the fingertips (which are the coolest part of the hands) until the whole bowl of ingredients looks like fresh breadcrumbs without any large pieces of fat to be seen. After remaining dry ingredients have been added, the mixture should be bound to a semi-stiff consistency with eggs and recommended liquid and stirred briskly with a fork without being beaten. The mixture should then be transferred to a greased cake tin (pan) lined with greased greaseproof (waxed) paper, banged gently up and down to disperse air bubbles and put straight into a pre-heated oven, on the centre shelf unless otherwise stated. Length of baking time is given in all recipes but to make doubly sure, a cocktail stick, skewer or fine knitting needle should be inserted into the centre before the cake is removed from the oven. If this comes out clean, then the cake is cooked.

A note here on fat. Margarine, lard or cooking fat (shortening) may be used in rubbed-in cakes, with equal success, but if preferred, a mixture of fats – such as half margarine and half lard – is just as good.

A few common faults

Cake heavy

1. If plain (all-purpose) flour used, not enough baking powder added.
2. Too much flour in proportion to fat.
3. Fat was warm and became oily as it was being rubbed in.

Family fruit cake

4. Too much liquid added.

5. Oven too cool.

Cake full of large holes

1. Fat not rubbed into flour finely enough.

2. Mixture beaten or over-stirred after eggs and liquid were added.

Cake crust hard and sugary

1. Too much sugar used.

2. Cake overcooked.

Small cakes (such as rock buns) spread

1. Mixture too soft

2. Baking tray (sheet) over-greased.

3. Oven too cool.

Large peaks in centre and/or top badly cracked

1. Oven too hot.

2. Cake too near top of oven.

3. Mixture too stiff.

4. Tin (pan) too small.

Fruit sunken

1. Fruit wet. If washed, must be thoroughly dried before adding to cake mixture.

2. Too much liquid added to dry ingredients resulting in over-soft mixture.

3. Too much baking powder used.

4. Oven not hot enough.

5. Opening and closing oven door while cake was rising.

Cake sinks in centre

1. Too much baking powder used.

2. Mixture too soft.

3. Oven too cool or too hot.

4. Cake under-cooked.

5. Opening and closing oven door while cake was rising.

Rock Buns

8 oz. (2 cups) self-raising
 flour

Dash of salt

$\frac{1}{2}$ level teaspoon *each* mixed spice and
 ground nutmeg

4 oz. ($\frac{1}{2}$ cup) lard, cooking fat (shortening),
 or margarine (or mixture of fats)

4 oz. (1 cup) currants

$3\frac{1}{2}$ oz. (just under $\frac{1}{2}$ cup) castor
 (granulated) sugar

1 dessertspoon (1 T) mixed chopped peel

1 standard egg, beaten

1–2 dessertspoons (2 T) cold milk to mix

Pre-heat oven to moderately hot (400°F, Gas Mark 6).

Sift the flour, salt and spices into bowl. Add the fat. Cut into the dry ingredients with a pastry cutter or round-topped knife, then rub in finely with fingertips. Add currants, sugar and peel. Toss the ingredients lightly together. Using a fork, mix to a *stiff* mixture with the beaten egg and milk.

Place 10–12 rocky mounds on a large, lightly greased baking tray (sheet), allowing room between each as they spread slightly.

Bake near the top of the oven for 15–20 minutes. Cool on a wire (cake) rack.

Store in an air-tight container when cold.

Mixed fruit buns

Make exactly as Rock Buns, substituting mixed dried fruit for the currants.

Plain Cup Cakes

8 oz. (2 cups) self-raising flour
Dash of salt
4 oz. ($\frac{1}{2}$ cup) lard, cooking fat (shortening), or margarine (or mixture of fats)
3$\frac{1}{2}$ oz. (just under $\frac{1}{2}$ cup) castor (granulated) or soft brown sugar
2$\frac{1}{2}$ oz. ($\frac{1}{2}$ cup) dried fruit
1 standard egg, beaten
1 teaspoon vanilla essence (extract)
About 5 tablespoons (6$\frac{1}{4}$ T) milk to mix

Pre-heat oven to moderately hot, (375°F, Gas Mark 5).

Stand 16–18 fluted paper cake cases in 16–18 ungreased bun tins (muffin cups).

Sift the flour and salt into bowl. Add the fat. Cut into dry ingredients with a pastry cutter or round-topped knife, then rub in finely.

Add the sugar and fruit.

Toss the ingredients lightly together. Using fork, mix to a softish batter with the egg, vanilla essence (extract) and milk, increasing milk by 1 or 2 teaspoons if the mixture seems stiff.

Spoon equal amounts into the paper cake cases and bake near the top of the oven for 15–20 minutes or until well risen, golden and firm. Cool on a wire (cake) rack. Store in an air-tight container when cold.

Orange or Lemon Cup Cakes

Make exactly as Plain Cup Cakes but omit the fruit. Add the finely grated peel of 1 small orange or 1 lemon with the sugar.

Coconut Cup Cakes

Make exactly as Plain Cup Cakes, but reduce the flour by 1 oz. ($\frac{1}{4}$ cup).

Add 1$\frac{1}{2}$ oz. (approximately $\frac{1}{2}$ cup) desiccated (dry flaked) coconut with the sugar.

Increase vanilla essence (extract) to 2 teaspoons.

Chocolate Cup Cakes

Make exactly as Plain Cup Cakes but reduce the flour by 1 oz. ($\frac{1}{4}$ cup). Replace with $\frac{1}{2}$ oz. (2 T) each cornflour (cornstarch) and cocoa powder. Sift with the flour and salt into bowl. Use soft brown sugar instead of castor (granulated).

Iced Cup Cakes

If liked, ice the Cup Cakes with glacé icing, made by sifting 8 oz. (about 1$\frac{1}{2}$ cups) icing (confectioner's) sugar into a bowl and adding water or fruit juice, teaspoon by teaspoon, until a fairly thick, smooth icing is formed. Spread evenly over the tops of cooked cakes and leave to set.

If liked, decorate by sprinkling with chocolate vermicelli or hundreds and thousands, or by topping with nuts, halved glacé cherries or chocolate buttons.

Cherry Cake

3 tablespoons (3$\frac{3}{4}$ T) glacé cherries
7 oz (1$\frac{3}{4}$ cups) plain (all-purpose) flour
$\frac{1}{4}$ level teaspoon salt
3 level teaspoons baking powder
1$\frac{1}{2}$ level tablespoons (just under 2 T) coarse semolina
4 oz. ($\frac{1}{2}$ cup) lard, cooking fat (shortening), or margarine (or mixture of fats)
3$\frac{1}{2}$ oz. (just under $\frac{1}{2}$ cup) castor (granulated) sugar
1–2 teaspoons vanilla essence (extract)
1 standard egg, beaten
6–8 tablespoons (7$\frac{1}{2}$–10 T) cold milk to mix

Pre-heat oven to moderate (350°F, Gas Mark 4). Brush a 6 in. round cake tin (pan) with melted fat. Line the base and sides with greaseproof (waxed) paper and brush the paper with more fat. Quarter the cherries. Wash to remove syrup then dry thoroughly. Sift the flour, salt and baking powder into bowl. Add the semolina. Cut the fat into the dry ingredients with a pastry cutter or round-topped knife, then rub in finely with fingertips. Add the cherries and sugar.

Toss the ingredients well together. Using a fork, mix to a semi-stiff batter with the vanilla essence (extract), egg and milk, stirring briskly without beating. Transfer to the prepared tin (pan) and bake in the centre of the oven for $1\frac{1}{4}$–$1\frac{1}{2}$ hours until well risen and golden, or until a cocktail stick etc. inserted into the centre of the cake comes out clean.

Leave in the tin (pan) for 10 minutes then turn out and cool on a wire (cake) rack. Peel away the paper and store the cake in an air-tight container when cold.

Austrian Style Hazelnut Jam Tart

4 oz. (1 cup) plain (all-purpose) flour
1 level teaspoon cinnamon
Dash of salt
4 oz. (1 cup) ground hazelnuts
$3\frac{1}{2}$ oz. (just under $\frac{1}{2}$ cup) castor (granulated) sugar
4 oz. ($\frac{1}{2}$ cup) butter, slightly softened
1 egg yolk
Raspberry jam
1 egg white
Icing (confectioner's) sugar for dusting, optional

Stand 7 in. fluted flan ring on a lightly greased baking tray (sheet).

Sift the flour, cinnamon and salt into a bowl. Add the hazelnuts and sugar. Add the butter. Cut into the dry ingredients with a pastry cutter or round-topped knife, then rub in lightly with fingertips. Add the egg yolk and stir in with knife. Draw the mixture together, handling as little as possible, and wrap in foil. Refrigerate for $1\frac{1}{2}$–2 hours.

Before making the tart, pre-heat the oven to warm (325°F, Gas Mark 3). Take two-thirds of the dough and press into the prepared flan ring, making sure that the dough round the base and sides is of even thickness. (It should be thicker than shortcrust pastry.) Fill with jam. Turn the remaining dough onto a floured surface and roll out fairly thinly. Cut into strips and criss-cross over the jam filling, pressing the ends of the strips well into the dough round the sides so that they hold in place.

Brush with lightly beaten egg white then bake in the centre of the oven for about $\frac{3}{4}$–1 hour or until golden.

Leave for 10 minutes then carefully lift off flan ring and transfer tart to a plate. If liked, dust lightly with sifted icing (confectioner's) sugar. Serve while still warm and accompany, if liked, with softly whipped cream.

Austrian style hazelnut jam tart

Walnut Ring

8 oz. (2 cups) self-raising flour
Dash of salt
4 oz. (½ cup) lard, cooking fat (shortening),
    or margarine (or mixture of fats)
4 oz. (1 cup) walnuts, finely chopped
4 oz. (½ cup) castor (granulated) sugar
1 standard egg, beaten
1 teaspoon vanilla essence (extract)
About 6–7 tablespoons (7½–8¾ T) cold
    milk to mix
Icing
4 oz. (1 cup) icing (confectioner's) sugar
Warm water or orange juice
Shelled walnut halves

Pre-heat oven to moderate (350°F, Gas Mark 4).
Brush a 7 in. ring tin (pan) heavily with melted fat.
Sift the flour and salt into a bowl. Add the fat. Cut into the dry ingredients with a pastry cutter or round-topped knife, then rub in finely with fingertips.
Add the nuts and sugar.
Toss the ingredients lightly together then, using a fork, mix to a semi-stiff batter with the egg, vanilla essence (extract) and milk, stirring briskly without beating.
Transfer to the prepared tin (pan) and bake in the centre of the oven for 1–1¼ hours or until well risen and firm.
Leave in the tin (pan) for 5 minutes, then turn out and cool on wire (cake) rack.
When completely cold, pour over glacé icing, made by mixing the sifted sugar to a thinnish but smooth icing with water or orange juice.
Top the cake with walnut halves when the icing is set.

Family Fruit Cake

8 oz. (2 cups) self-raising flour
Dash of salt
4 oz. (½ cup) lard, cooking fat (shortening),
    or margarine (or mixture of fats)
3½ oz. (just under ½ cup) castor
    (granulated) sugar
5 oz. (1 cup) mixed (chopped) dried fruit
1 level teaspoon finely grated orange peel
1 standard egg, beaten
About 6-7 tablespoons (7½–8¾ T) cold milk
    to mix

Pre-heat oven to moderate, (350°F, Gas Mark 4).
Brush a 1 lb. loaf tin (2 cup capacity oblong loaf pan) or 6 in. round cake tin (pan) with melted fat.

Line the base and sides with greaseproof (waxed) paper.
Brush the paper with more fat.
Sift the flour and salt into bowl. Add the fat. Cut into the dry ingredients with a pastry cutter or round-topped knife, then rub in finely with fingertips.
Add sugar, fruit and orange peel.
Toss the ingredients lightly together. Using a fork, mix to a semi-stiff batter with the egg and milk, stirring briskly without beating.
When evenly combined, transfer to the prepared tin (pan).
Bake just above the centre of the oven for 1–1¼ hours until well risen and golden or until a cocktail stick etc. inserted into the centre of the cake comes out clean.
Leave in the tin (pan) for 20 minutes, then turn out and cool on a wire (cake) rack. Peel away the paper and store the cake in an air-tight container when cold.

Farmhouse Cake

Make exactly as Family Fruit Cake but add 12 washed, dried and chopped glacé cherries and 2 oz. (½ cup) mixed chopped peel with the other fruit.

Date and Walnut Cake

Make exactly as Family Fruit Cake, but omit the dried fruit and add the same amount of chopped dates and 2 oz. (½ cup) coarsely chopped walnuts. If liked, use soft brown sugar instead of castor (granulated), or half and half.

Coconut Cake

Make exactly as Family Fruit Cake but omit fruit. Reduce the flour by 1 oz. (¼ cup). Add 1½ oz. (½ cup) desiccated (dry flaked) coconut with the sugar. Add 1 teaspoon vanilla essence (extract) with the egg and milk.

Spicy Fruit Cake

Make exactly as Family Fruit Cake but sift the flour and salt with 1–2 level teaspoons mixed spice.

Plain Chocolate Cake

Make exactly as Family Fruit Cake but reduce the flour by 1 oz. (¼ cup). Replace with 1 oz. (¼ cup) cocoa powder; sift into bowl with flour and salt. Use soft brown sugar instead of castor (granulated) and omit the fruit completely. Add 1–2 teaspoons vanilla essence (extract) with the egg and milk.

Raisin Orange Cake

Make exactly as Family Fruit Cake, substituting seedless raisins (chopped if large) for mixed fruit. Add the finely grated peel of 1 small orange with the raisins and sugar. Mix the dry ingredients with egg, 3 tablespoons ($3\frac{3}{4}$ T) milk and about 3 tablespoons ($3\frac{3}{4}$ T) fresh, strained orange juice.

Plain Ginger Cake

Make exactly as Family Fruit Cake but sift the flour and salt into bowl with 2–3 level teaspoons ground ginger. If liked, add 2–3 level tablespoons ($2\frac{1}{2}$–$3\frac{3}{4}$ T) finely chopped preserved ginger (well washed and dried first) with sugar.

Basic Shortbread

4 oz. (1 cup) plain (all-purpose) flour
Dash of salt
4 level tablespoons fine semolina
2 oz. (4 T) castor (granulated) sugar
4 oz. ($\frac{1}{2}$ cup) butter or margarine (the latter preferably with a percentage of butter)
Castor (granulated) sugar for dusting

Pre-heat oven to warm (325°F, Gas Mark 3). Sift the flour, salt and semolina into a bowl. Add the sugar and butter or margarine. Cut into the dry ingredients with a pastry cutter or round-topped knife, then rub in to form crumbly mixture.

Draw together, knead lightly then press smoothly into a 7 in. ungreased sandwich tin (layer cake pan) or a fluted flan ring standing on a greased baking tray (sheet). Ensure the shortbread mixture is evenly distributed, then prick lightly with a fork.

Bake in the centre of the oven for 35–45 minutes or until the colour of pale straw.

Leave in the tin (pan) for about 5 minutes (or lift off flan ring), then cut into 8 wedges with a knife. Remove carefully from the tin (pan) and transfer to a wire cooling (cake) rack. Dust lightly with extra castor (granulated) sugar and store in an air-tight container when cold.

Dutch Style Butter Cake

8 oz. (2 cups) self-raising flour
Dash of salt
1 level teaspoon cinnamon
2 oz. ($\frac{1}{4}$ cup) soft brown sugar
6 oz. ($\frac{3}{4}$ cup) Dutch butter, slightly softened
1 egg, separated

Pre-heat oven to warm (325°F, Gas Mark 3). Sift the flour, salt and cinnamon into a bowl. Add the sugar and toss ingredients lightly together to mix. Cut in the butter with a pastry cutter or round-topped knife, then rub into dry

ingredients with fingertips. Stir in the egg yolk, then draw mixture together with knife.

Knead lightly then press into a 7 in. square tin (pan). Prick with a fork and brush with lightly beaten egg white.

Bake in the centre of the oven for 35–45 minutes or until golden. Leave for 10 minutes. Cut into squares, remove from the tin (pan) and cool on a wire (cake) rack. Store in air-tight container when cold.

Almond Butter Cake

To vary, stud the top of butter cake with zig-zag rows of blanched and halved almonds before brushing with egg white.

Pull-apart Cake

1½ oz. (1 cup) cornflakes, crushed
1 level teaspoon finely grated orange peel
10 oz. (2½ cups) self-raising flour
½ level teaspoon salt
2 oz. (4 T) castor (granulated) sugar
2 oz. (¼ cup) cooking fat (shortening)
2 oz. (¼ cup) butter
1 standard egg, beaten
6 tablespoons (¾ cup) milk
4 level tablespoons (5 T) clear honey

Icing
4 oz. (¾ cup) icing (confectioner's) sugar
3 dessertspoons (3 T) milk
½ teaspoon vanilla essence (extract)

Pre-heat oven to moderately hot (375°F, Gas Mark 5). Well grease 2 lb. loaf tin (4 cup capacity oblong loaf pan). Line base and sides with greased greaseproof (waxed) paper.

Mix the cornflakes and orange peel together and keep on one side.

Sift the flour and salt into a bowl. Add the sugar, cooking fat (shortening) and butter. With a pastry cutter or round-topped knife, cut the fats into the dry ingredients, then rub in finely with fingertips. Add the egg and milk and lightly stir until well mixed.

Turn the mixture on to a floured surface and knead lightly. With floured hands, shape the mixture into thirty 1 in. balls.

Place half the dough balls in the prepared tin (pan) and coat with 2 tablespoons (2½ T) honey. Sprinkle over half the cornflake mixture then place the remaining dough balls on top. Spoon over the remaining honey, then sprinkle with the remaining cornflake mixture.

Bake in the centre of the oven for about 35–45 minutes, until lightly brown and cooked through, or until cocktail stick etc. inserted into the centre comes out clean. Leave in the tin (pan) for 5 minutes then turn out and cool on wire (cake) racks. Peel away the paper.

To make icing: sift the sugar into a bowl, gradually stir in the milk and vanilla essence (extract). Stir briskly until smooth. Spoon over the cake and serve warm.

Refrigerator nut cookies
1 : Drawing mixture together with fingertips

Ginger Shortie

6 oz. (1½ cups) self-raising flour
4 level teaspoons ground ginger
4 oz. (½ cup) butter
3 oz. (6 T) castor (granulated) sugar
1 standard egg
2 tablespoons ginger or orange
**   marmalade (preserves)**
6 oz. (1½ cups) icing (confectioner's) sugar,
**   sifted**
Strained orange juice or water
Crystallized ginger or glacé cherries

Pre-heat oven to moderate (350°F, Gas Mark 4).
Grease and paper line a deep, 7 in. round sandwich tin (pan).
Sift the flour with the ginger. Cut in the butter with a pastry cutter or round-topped knife, then rub in with fingertips. Add the sugar and enough beaten egg to bind mixture together.
Turn onto a lightly floured surface, divide in half and knead quickly. Roll into two 7 in. circles. Place one circle in the tin (pan), spread with marmalade (preserves) then lift the other circle on top.
Bake in the centre of the oven for about 50 minutes until golden brown. Leave in the tin (pan) about 5 minutes then turn on to a rack.
Mix the icing (confectioner's) sugar with just enough water or orange juice to make a thickish and smooth icing. Spread over the top of the shortcake. Decorate with crystallized ginger or glacé cherries. Cut into pieces before serving.

Refrigerator Nut Cookies

8 oz. (2 cups) plain (all-purpose) flour
4 level tablespoons (5 T) semolina
6 oz. (¾ cup) butter or margarine

2 : Forming cookie mixture into rolls

5 oz. (10 T) castor (granulated) sugar
1 egg yolk mixed with 2 dessertspoons (2 T)
**   cold water**
1 egg white
3 oz. (¾ cup) shelled walnut halves

Sift the flour and semolina into a bowl. Add the fat, cut into the dry ingredients with a pastry cutter or round-topped knife then rub in finely with fingertips. Add the sugar, toss the ingredients lightly together, then mix to a stiff paste with the egg yolk and water.
Draw together with fingertips, turn out on to a floured board and divide in half. Shape each piece into a smooth roll, wrap in greaseproof (waxed) paper and chill until firm, about 2–3 hours.
Unwrap, then cut the rolls into very thin slices. Transfer to greased baking trays (sheets), brush with lightly beaten egg white and top with a small piece of walnut.
Bake in the centre of a moderately hot oven (400°F, Gas Mark 6) for 8–10 minutes or until golden. Cool on a wire (cake) rack and store in an air-tight container when completely cold.
Makes approximately 7 dozen cookies.
Note: Not all the cookies need be baked together. If, for example, only a couple of dozen are needed, simply remove one of the rolls from the refrigerator, cut off 24 slices and bake as directed. Re-wrap rest of roll and refrigerate until required.

Afternoon Tea Scones

8 oz. (2 cups) self-raising flour
1 level teaspoon baking powder
Pinch of salt
2 oz. (¼ cup) butter or table margarine
1 level tablespoon (1¼ T) castor
**   (granulated) sugar**
¼ pint (⅝ cup) cold milk

3 : Slicing refrigerated cookie roll

4 : Baked cookies

Pre-heat oven to very hot (450°F, Gas Mark 8). Sift the flour, baking powder and salt into a bowl. Cut the fat into the dry ingredients with a pastry cutter or round-topped knife then rub in finely with fingertips. Add the sugar and toss the ingredients lightly together. Mix to a soft but not sticky dough with the milk.

Knead quickly and lightly on a floured surface until smooth, then roll out to about $1\frac{1}{2}$ in. thickness. Cut into 16–18 rounds with a $1\frac{3}{4}$–2 in. fluted biscuit cutter dipped in flour. Lightly re-knead, re-roll and cut trimmings.

Transfer to a greased baking tray (sheet) and if liked, brush tops with beaten egg or milk. Bake near the top of the oven for 8–10 minutes or until well-risen and golden.

Transfer to a wire (cake) rack and leave until lukewarm before splitting each scone in half with fingers. (Do not cut scones as this makes them doughy.) Spread with butter or table margarine and accompany with jam (preserves), honey, syrup, treacle or lemon curd.

Wholemeal Scones

Make exactly as above but use half self-raising flour and half wholemeal (wholewheat) flour. Increase baking powder to 2 level teaspoons.

Strawberry or Peach Shortcake

Make the scone mixture as above. Roll out dough 1 in. thick and cut into 6 rounds with a $3\frac{1}{2}$–4 in. cutter.

Transfer to a greased baking tray (sheet) and bake near the top of a hot oven (425°F, Gas Mark 7) for 15–20 minutes.

Cool to lukewarm on wire (cake) rack, split open with fingers and butter thickly. Sandwich together, in pairs, with sliced strawberries (sprinkled with sugar) or well-drained canned peach slices. Top each shortcake with a dollop of softly whipped cream.

Makes about 6.

Tea time Scone Round

8 oz. (2 cups) self-raising flour
1 level teaspoon baking powder
Dash of salt
2 oz. ($\frac{1}{4}$ cup) butter or table margarine
2 oz. ($\frac{1}{4}$ cup) castor (granulated) sugar
$2\frac{1}{2}$ oz. ($\frac{1}{2}$ cup) mixed (chopped) dried fruit
1 standard egg
Cold milk

Pre-heat oven to hot (425°F, Gas Mark 7). Sift the flour, baking powder and salt into a bowl. Cut the fat into the dry ingredients with a pastry cutter or round-topped knife then rub in with fingertips. Add the sugar and fruit and toss ingredients lightly together.

Beat the egg in a measuring cup then make up to $\frac{1}{4}$ pint ($\frac{5}{8}$ cup) with cold milk. Add to the dry ingredients all at once and, using knife, quickly mix to a soft but not sticky dough.

Turn out on to floured surface, knead quickly until smooth then pat or roll into an 8 in. round. Transfer to a greased baking tray (sheet) and mark into wedges by indenting with back of knife. Bake near the top of the oven for 15–20 minutes or until well-risen and golden. Leave to cool about 10 minutes then separate into wedges. Split each wedge when almost cold, spread thickly with butter and serve at once.

Norfolk scone

Afternoon Tea Ring

Make up exactly as previous recipe. Divide mixture into 8 equally sized pieces and lightly cut each into a round. Stand in an overlapping ring on greased baking tray (sheet). Brush with a little beaten egg and bake just above the centre of a hot oven (425°F, Gas Mark 7) for 20–25 minutes or until golden. Cool on a wire (cake) rack.

Norfolk Scone

1 lb. (4 cups) self-raising flour
2 level teaspoons salt
4 oz. ($\frac{1}{2}$ cup) butter or margarine
2 standard eggs, beaten
$\frac{1}{4}$ pint ($\frac{5}{8}$ cup) milk + 4 tablespoons (5 T)

Filling
1 oz. (2 T) softened butter or margarine
4 oz. (1 cup) currants
$\frac{1}{2}$ level teaspoon grated nutmeg
4 oz. ($\frac{1}{2}$ cup) demerara sugar
Milk

Pre-heat oven to moderately hot (400°F, Gas Mark 6).
Sift together the flour and salt. Add the butter or margarine. Cut into the dry ingredients with a pastry cutter or round-topped knife then rub in with fingertips. Mix to a soft dough with the eggs and milk.
Turn on to a floured surface and knead lightly. Divide in half and roll each out into an 8 in. circle about $\frac{3}{4}$ in. thick.
Lift one circle on to a greased baking tray (sheet) and spread with butter. Mix the currants, nutmeg and three-quarters of the sugar together and sprinkle over the butter. Place the second circle on top and mark into 10 wedges. Brush with milk and sprinkle with remaining sugar.
Bake in the centre of the oven for about 50 minutes. Leave for about 10 minutes, cut into wedges and serve while still warm.

American Style Ring Doughnuts

12 oz. (3 cups) self-raising flour
1 level teaspoon salt
1 level teaspoon cinnamon
4 oz. ($\frac{1}{2}$ cup) butter, margarine or cooking fat (shortening)
2 oz. ($\frac{1}{4}$ cup) castor (granulated) sugar
1 standard egg, beaten
$\frac{1}{4}$ pint ($\frac{5}{8}$ cup) cold milk + 2 tablespoons ($2\frac{1}{2}$ T)
Deep fat or oil for frying
Extra castor (granulated) sugar for tossing

Sift the flour, salt and cinnamon into bowl. Cut the fat into the dry ingredients with a pastry cutter or round-topped knife then rub in with fingertips. Add the sugar and toss ingredients lightly together. Using knife, mix to a soft but not sticky dough with the beaten egg and milk. Turn out on to a lightly floured board and knead quickly until smooth. Roll out to $\frac{1}{2}$ in. thick and cut into rounds with a 2 in. plain biscuit cutter. Remove the centres with a 1 in. cutter then re-roll trimmings and cut into more rings.
Fry, a few at a time, in hot fat or oil for about 3–4 minutes, turning once. Remove from pan, drain on soft kitchen (absorbent) paper and toss in sugar.
Makes about 20.

Richer cakes and gâteaux

These are richer concoctions altogether than the cakes and cookies in the previous section, and form all manner of delicious and intriguing variations. Into this category fall many of the more popular cakes: Victoria sandwiches filled with jam and sometimes whipped cream or butter cream; frosted coffee gateau with walnuts; Madeira cake capped with its familiar curl of citron peel; almond-studded Dundee; moist and fruity Genoa; light-as-air fairy and butterfly cakes and coconut encrusted Madeleines. Chocolatey Devil's Food Cake, two-toned Battenburg (cosily wrapped in marzipan), and crumbly Seedcake – which is either loved or loathed – are three more in the same repertoire, as are all sorts of mouth-watering cakes and gateaux. Recipes for all these are included in this section.

In the days before food mixers, easy-cream margarines and whipped-up cooking fats, creamed cakes required more time, more patience, more dedication and, to be strictly honest, more skill. Now, with such a host of modern innovations around us, they are basically not much more complicated or difficult to make than rubbed-in cakes. Again, the essential things to remember for successful results are that all ingredients should be at room temperature and never taken straight from the refrigerator, that the oven should be pre-heated, and that the cakes be baked on the centre shelf unless otherwise stated. These cakes respond badly to the oven door being opened and closed while they are rising and to any sort of manhandling while they are still warm; they are less sturdy than rubbed-in cakes and require a lighter touch!

Creamed cakes are richer than rubbed-in ones because the proportion of fat and sugar to flour is higher (as will be seen from the recipes), and as a general rule more eggs are also used – often, one to every 2 oz. ($\frac{1}{2}$ cup) unsifted flour. As the proportion of fat, sugar and eggs to flour increases (resulting in more air being incorporated into the mixture) so there is a decrease in the amount of raising agent required; thus many of the recipes for large cakes call for plain flour (all-purpose) instead of self-raising, with varying amounts of baking powder or, in some instances, none at all. It is the air, beaten into the mixture while creaming, plus the eggs – which act as the raising agent – that give a light-textured, melt-in-the-mouth cake.

Despite recipe books and detailed instructions, those making a rich cake for the first time can go wrong if they underestimate the time needed for proper creaming. With a wooden spoon and conventional fats, it can take anything from 5–10 minutes, depending on strength of arm and determination! With a mixer, half the time. The fat (which may be a mixture of margarine and butter, margarine and white fat or butter and white fat) should be creamed with the sugar until the whole thing looks like a light fluffy mass of softly whipped cream, and not much deeper in colour either. The eggs should be added whole, one at a time, with a dessertspoon (spoonful) of sifted dry ingredients and beaten in *thoroughly*. The small amount of flour mixture with each egg, plus the beating, stops the creamed fat and sugar separating and curdling, a factor which could cause heaviness of texture in the finished cake. After stirring in further additions such as fruit, nuts and flavourings, the beating has to stop and the dry ingredients must be stirred gently into the mixture with a large metal spoon.

Tins (pans) for these cakes should be brushed with melted white cooking fat

(shortening), margarine or unsalted butter, the base and sides lined with greaseproof (waxed) paper and then the paper brushed again with fat. When baked and removed from the oven, the cakes should be left in the tins (pans) to firm-up for between 5 and 15 minutes (depending on size and richness) before being turned out on to a wire (cake) rack. As soon as they are completely cold, the cakes may be filled, iced and decorated as directed or, if left completely unadorned, stored in an air-tight container until required.

A note here, once again, about fat. It should be soft to the touch but *not* runny and beginning to oil.

For speed

If you have to make a creamed cake in a hurry and the basic ingredients are still in the fridge, stand the mixing bowl in a sink containing a little hot water, add the fat in small pieces and allow it to soften, stirring frequently. Put the egg or eggs into a small bowl and cover with hot water – this brings them fairly quickly to room temperature.

Mandarin mocha cake

A few common faults

See those listed under rubbed-in cakes. In addition, the following apply to cakes made by the creaming method.

Close texture and heavy
1. Fat and sugar insufficiently creamed
2. Creamed mixture not beaten adequately after each egg was added.
3. Not enough raising agent added.
4. Too much flour used
5. Oven too hot or too cold

Texture full of holes
1. Dry ingredients beaten into creamed mixture instead of being folded in.
2. Dry ingredients not evenly distributed.
3. Tin (pan) not banged gently up and down to disperse air bubbles before baking.

Victoria Sandwich Cake (1)

4 oz. (1 cup) self-raising flour
Dash of salt
4 oz. ($\frac{1}{2}$ cup) mixture margarine and
  butter, or other combination
4 oz. ($\frac{1}{2}$ cup) castor (granulated) sugar
1 teaspoon vanilla essence (extract)
2 standard eggs

Pre-heat oven to moderate (350°F, Gas Mark 4). Brush two 7 in. round sandwich tins (cake pans) with melted fat. Line bases with rounds of greaseproof (waxed) paper and brush paper with more fat.

Sift the flour and salt into a bowl.

Put the fat, sugar and vanilla essence into another bowl and cream until light and fluffy. Beat in the whole eggs, one at a time, adding a dessertspoon (tablespoon) sifted dry ingredients with each. Fold in remaining flour with a large metal spoon.

Divide mixture equally between the prepared tins (pans). Spread evenly with a knife then tap the tins (pans) gently to disperse air bubbles. Bake in the centre of the oven for 25–30 minutes or until well risen and golden. Remove from the oven and leave in tins (pans) for 5 minutes.

Turn out and cool on a wire rack.

When completely cold, sandwich together with jam (preserves) and sprinkle with a little sifted icing (confectioner's) sugar or castor (granulated) sugar

Cream-filled Victoria Sandwich

Make exactly as above. Fill with jam (preserves) plus whipped cream or butter cream.

To make a simple butter cream, beat 2 oz. ($\frac{1}{4}$ cup) butter until very soft. Gradually beat in 3–4 oz. ($\frac{1}{2}$–$\frac{5}{8}$ cup) sifted icing (confectioner's) sugar and continue beating until light and fluffy. If liked, flavour to taste with vanilla.

Chocolate sandwich cake 1 : Sifting dry ingredients *2 : Adding eggs*
3 : Beating in eggs *4 : Folding in dry ingredients*

Victoria Sandwich Cake (2)

This is the one-bowl version of the traditional recipe.

Make exactly as Victoria Sandwich Cake (1), but sift the flour and salt with 1 level teaspoon baking powder, and use luxury or easy-cream margarine or whipped-up cooking fat (or combination).

Put all the ingredients in a bowl and beat for approximately 3–4 minutes or until creamy. Divide between prepared tins (pans) and bake as directed.

Coffee Nut Sandwich

Make exactly as Victoria Sandwich Cake (1) and (2). Add 1 oz. (¼ cup) finely chopped walnuts after beating in eggs in version (1) or add to rest of ingredients in version (2).

When cold, slice each cake in half horizontally and sandwich together with ½ pint (1¼ cups) whipped double cream (whipping cream), flavoured to taste with sifted icing (confectioner's) sugar and a little strong coffee or liquid coffee essence (extract). Spread the remaining cream over the top of the cake and decorate with walnut halves.

If preferred, fill and ice the cake with coffee butter cream, made by beating 6 oz. (¾ cup) butter until very soft then gradually beating in

5 : Finished cake

12 oz. (2 cups) sifted icing (confectioner's) sugar and about 2 tablespoons (2½ T) liquid coffee essence (extract).

Orange or Lemon Sandwich

Make exactly as Victoria Sandwich Cake (1) or (2), but omit the vanilla essence (extract) and replace with 2 level teaspoons finely grated orange or lemon peel.

Sandwich together with lemon curd and dust with sifted icing (confectioner's) sugar.

Chocolate Sandwich Cake

5 oz. (1¼ cups) self-raising flour
1 oz. vanilla flavoured custard powder
  (¼ cup cornstarch + 1 teaspoon vanilla extract)
1 oz. (¼ cup) cocoa powder
6 oz. (¾ cup) butter or margarine (or mixture), softened
6 oz. (¾ cup) castor (granulated) sugar
3 standard eggs
2 tablespoons (2½ T) milk

Pre-heat oven to moderate (350°F, Gas Mark 4). Brush two 8 in. sandwich tins (cake pans) with melted fat. Line bases with rounds of greased greaseproof (waxed) paper.

Sift the flour, custard powder (cornstarch) and cocoa together twice. Cream the butter or margarine and sugar together until light and fluffy, then beat in the whole eggs, one at a time, adding a dessertspoon (tablespoon) sifted dry ingredients with each. (If using cornstarch, beat in 1 teaspoon vanilla extract with the egg.) Fold in half the remaining flour mixture with a large metal spoon, stir in the milk then fold in the remaining flour.

Divide equally between the prepared tins (pans) and bake in the centre of the oven for 30–35 minutes or until well risen and firm. Leave in the tins (pans) for 5 minutes, then turn out on to a wire (cake) rack. When cold, sandwich together with chocolate butter cream.

Chocolate Butter Cream
3 oz. (⅓ cup) icing (confectioner's) sugar
1 level dessertspoon (1 T) cocoa powder
2 oz. (¼ cup) butter
½ teaspoon vanilla essence (extract)
1 dessertspoon (1 T) hot water

Sift the sugar and cocoa together, then cream with the butter till light in texture and pale in colour. Add the vanilla essence (extract) and water and beat in thoroughly.

Rich Cup Cakes

Make up Victoria Sandwich mixture (1) or (2) (see page 24–5).

Put equal amounts in 20–24 fluted paper cake cases standing in ungreased bun tins (muffin cups). Bake just above the centre of a moderately hot oven (375°F, Gas Mark 5) for approximately 20 minutes or until well risen and golden. Cool on a wire (cake) rack.

Butterfly Cakes

Make and bake Rich Cup Cakes as above. To make 'butterflies', cut a slice off the top of each cake, then cut in half to form two wings. Pipe a heavy line of butter cream on top of each cake then put halved slices into cream, angled to form wings. Dust with sifted icing (confectioner's) sugar.

Butter Cream

Beat 2 oz. ($\frac{1}{4}$ cup) butter until soft then gradually beat in 4 oz. (just under 1 cup) sifted icing (confectioner's) sugar and vanilla essence (extract) to taste.

Fairy Cakes

Make exactly as Rich Cup Cakes but add 3–4 level tablespoons (4–5 T) currants after beating in eggs.

Assorted Rich Cup Cakes

Make up Victoria Sandwich mixture (1) or (2) (see page 24–5). After beating in eggs and before folding in dry ingredients, add chosen flavouring or essence: 1–2 level teaspoons grated orange or lemon peel; 1 oz. ($\frac{1}{4}$ cup) chopped nuts; 1–2 level tablespoons ($1\frac{1}{4}$–$2\frac{1}{2}$ T) chocolate dots; 1–3 level tablespoons ($1\frac{1}{4}$–$3\frac{3}{4}$ T) mixed (chopped) dried fruit; 2–3 level tablespoons ($2\frac{1}{2}$–$3\frac{3}{4}$ T) well washed, dried and finely chopped glacé cherries. When baked, either leave plain or dust with sifted icing (confectioner's) sugar.

Slab Cake

Make up Victoria Sandwich mixture (1) or (2) (see page 24–5) using 6 oz. ($1\frac{1}{2}$ cups) self-raising flour, a dash of salt, 6 oz. ($\frac{3}{4}$ cup) castor (granulated) sugar, 6 oz. ($\frac{3}{4}$ cup) fat and 3 standard eggs. Spread the mixture into a greased and paper-lined Swiss roll tin (jelly roll pan) measuring about 11 × 8 × $1\frac{1}{2}$ in. Bake in the centre of a moderate oven (350°F, Gas Mark 4) for about 20–25 minutes. Leave in the tin (pan) for 5 minutes before turning out and cooling on a wire (cake) rack.

Square Sandwich Cake

Cut Slab Cake in half so that each piece measures about $5\frac{1}{2}$ × 8 in. and sandwich together with jam (preserves) etc. to taste. Dust with castor (granulated) sugar or sifted icing (confectioner's) sugar.

Iced Fancies

Make Slab Cake as above.

When cold, cut into fancy shapes with cutters, or into fingers, squares, diamonds, rounds or ovals. Spread tops with glacé icing, whipped cream or butter cream, then decorate with nuts, halved glacé cherries, angelica, chocolate drops (pieces) or dots, chocolate vermicelli or crystallized flower petals.

Coconut Squares

Make Slab Cake as above.

When cold, cut into cubes. Brush all over with melted plum or apricot jam (preserves), then toss in desiccated (dry flaked) coconut.

Madeleines

Make up Victoria Sandwich mixture (1) or (2) (see page 24–5).

Divide equally between 12 well greased castle pudding or dariole moulds (chimney-shaped individual pans). Bake in the centre of a moderate oven (350°F, Gas Mark 4) for 20–25 minutes or until well-risen and golden. Leave in tins (moulds) for 5 minutes, then turn out on to a wire rack. When completely cold, cut a slice off the wide part of each Madeleine so that it stands upright. Brush top and sides of cakes with melted apricot jam (preserves), then roll in desiccated (dry flaked) coconut. Top each with half a glacé cherry and 2 angelica leaves.

Basic Madeira Cake

8 oz. (2 cups) plain (all-purpose) flour
2 level teaspoons baking powder
$\frac{1}{4}$ level teaspoon salt
6 oz. ($\frac{3}{4}$ cup) butter or margarine, softened
6 oz. ($\frac{3}{4}$ cup) castor (granulated) sugar
Finely grated peel of 1 small lemon (optional)
1 teaspoon vanilla essence (extract)
3 standard eggs
2 tablespoons ($2\frac{1}{2}$ T) cold milk
1 strip crystallized citron peel (optional)

Pre-heat oven to warm (325°F, Gas Mark 3). Brush a 7 in. round cake tin (pan) or 2 lb. loaf tin (4 cup capacity oblong loaf pan) with melted

Caraway seed cake

fat. Sift together flour, baking powder and salt. Cream the butter or margarine, sugar, lemon peel (if used) and vanilla essence (extract) together until light and fluffy then beat in the whole eggs, one at a time, adding a dessertspoon (tablespoon) sifted dry ingredients with each. Using a metal spoon, fold in the rest of the dry ingredients alternately with milk.

When eventually combined, transfer to the prepared tin (pan) and smooth evenly with a knife. Place a strip of citron peel (if used) on top of the cake. Bake in the centre of the oven for $1\frac{1}{2}$–$1\frac{3}{4}$ hours or until well risen and golden, or until a cocktail stick etc. inserted into the centre comes out clean.

Leave in the tin (pan) for 10 minutes before turning out on to a wire (cake) rack. Carefully peel off the paper. Store in an air-tight container when cold.

Rich Madeira Cake

Make exactly as Basic Madeira, reducing baking powder to $\frac{1}{2}$ level teaspoon only. Use 8 oz. (1 cup) fat and 8 oz. (1 cup) castor (granulated) sugar, 4 standard eggs, and lemon peel and vanilla essence (extract) as directed. Omit milk completely. Bake in the centre of the oven at the same temperature, allowing 10–20 minutes extra baking time.

Caraway Seed Cake

Make Basic or Rich Madeira Cake omitting the grated lemon peel. Add 4–6 level teaspoons caraway seeds. Do *not* add citron peel.

Marble Cake

Make exactly as Rich Madeira Cake (see above) but after beating in the eggs, divide the mixture in 2 equal portions. Fold half the sifted flour into one portion. Add 1 level tablespoon ($1\frac{1}{4}$ T) sifted cocoa powder to remaining dry ingredients and fold into the second portion of creamed mixture alternately with 1 dessertspoon (1 T) milk. Drop alternate spoons of both mixtures into tin (pan) and bake as directed.

Genoa Cake

Make Basic or Rich Madeira Cake as above. After beating in the eggs, sugar, lemon peel and vanilla essence (extract), add 8 oz. ($1\frac{1}{2}$ cups) currants and raisins, 3 oz. ($\frac{1}{2}$ cup) mixed chopped peel, 2 tablespoons ($2\frac{1}{2}$ T) washed, dried and chopped glacé cherries and 1 oz. ($\frac{1}{4}$ cup) blanched and finely chopped almonds.

Bake in the centre of a cool oven (300°F, Gas Mark 2) for about 2–$2\frac{1}{2}$ hours. Leave in the tin (pan) for 15 minutes before turning out on to a wire (cake) rack. Store in an air-tight container when cold.

Fruit and nut loaf (left) Rich cherry cake (above)

Fruit and Nut Loaf

Make Basic or Rich Madeira Cake. After beating in the eggs, sugar, lemon peel and vanilla essence (extract), stir in 8 oz. (1½ cups) mixed (chopped) dried fruit.

Transfer to a greased and paper-lined 2 lb. loaf tin (4 cup capacity oblong loaf pan). Cover with about 2 level tablespoons (2½ T) blanched almonds, cut into thin slivers. Bake as above.

Rich Cherry Cake

3 tablespoons (3¾ T) glacé cherries
6 oz. (1½ cups) plain (all-purpose) flour
1 level teaspoon baking powder
¼ level teaspoon salt
2 level tablespoons (2½ T) fine semolina
1 oz. (2 T) ground almonds
4 oz. (½ cup) butter or margarine, softened
4 oz. (½ cup) castor (granulated) sugar
1 teaspoon vanilla or almond essence
  (extract)
2 standard eggs
3 tablespoons (3¾ T) milk

Pre-heat oven to moderate (350°F, Gas Mark 4). Brush a 7 in. round cake tin (pan) with melted fat. Line the base and sides with greaseproof (waxed) paper and brush the paper with more fat.

Halve the glacé cherries, then wash and dry thoroughly.

Sift together the flour, baking powder, salt and semolina. Stir in the ground almonds.

Cream the butter or margarine with the sugar and essence (extract) until light and fluffy, then beat in the whole eggs, one at a time, adding a dessertspoon (tablespoon) dry ingredients with each. Stir in the cherries then, using a large metal spoon, gently and lightly fold in the remaining dry ingredients alternately with milk.

Transfer to the prepared tin (pan) and bake in the centre of the oven for 1½–1¾ hours until well risen and golden, or until a cocktail stick etc. inserted into the centre comes out clean.

Leave in the tin (pan) for 10–15 minutes before turning out on to a wire (cake) rack. Carefully peel away the paper and store in an air-tight container when completely cold.

Dundee Cake

Make exactly as Rich Madeira Cake (see page 27), but use the finely grated peel of 1 small orange instead of lemon. After beating in the eggs, stir in 2 oz. ($\frac{1}{4}$ cup) ground almonds, 12 oz. ($2\frac{1}{2}$ cups) mixed (chopped) dried fruit and 2 oz. (just under $\frac{1}{2}$ cup) mixed chopped peel.

Transfer to the prepared tin (pan) and cover the top with rings of blanched split almonds.

Bake in the centre of a cool oven (300°F, Gas Mark 2) for 2–2$\frac{1}{2}$ hours until well risen and golden, or until a cocktail stick etc. inserted into the centre comes out clean.

Leave in the tin (pan) for 15–20 minutes before turning out on to a wire (cake) rack. Carefully peel away the paper. Store in an air-tight container when cold.

Chocolate Frosted Loaf

Make Basic or Rich Madeira Cake (see page 27), omitting the grated lemon peel. Bake in a 2 lb. greased and paper-lined loaf tin, (4 cup capacity oblong loaf pan). When completely cold, cover top with Chocolate Frosting, swirling it quickly with a knife.

Chocolate Frosting
6 oz. (1 cup firmly packed) soft brown sugar (light in colour)
2 oz. ($\frac{1}{4}$ cup) butter or table margarine
3 level tablespoons ($3\frac{3}{4}$ T) cocoa powder
1 teaspoon vanilla essence (extract)
3 tablespoons ($3\frac{3}{4}$ T) single (light) cream

Put all the ingredients in a saucepan. Stir over a gentle heat until the sugar dissolves. Increase the heat and bring the mixture to the boil, stirring continuously. Stop stirring, then boil briskly for exactly 3 minutes. Remove from heat. Cool slightly, then stand the saucepan in a bowl or sink containing some cold water. Beat with a rotary beater or whisk until icing thickens and is of spreadable consistency (which happens fairly rapidly). Spread over cake immediately.

Chocolate Layer Loaf

Make up Basic or Rich Madeira Cake mixture (see page 27) and bake in a loaf tin (pan) as directed for Chocolate Frosted Loaf (above). When cold, slice loaf twice lengthwise, then sandwich and coat the top and sides with *Chocolate Icing*: 2 oz. ($\frac{1}{4}$ cup) table or luxury margarine in 6 tablespoons ($7\frac{1}{2}$ T) water, gradually combine with 4 level tablespoons (5 T) cocoa powder, and then beat into 1 lb. ($3\frac{1}{2}$ cups) sifted icing (confectioner's) sugar until the

icing is smooth and well combined.

If preferred, *Chocolate Glacé Icing* may be used instead: melt 4 oz. (4 squares) broken plain (bitter) chocolate, 2 tablespoons ($2\frac{1}{2}$ T) water and 1 oz. (2 T) butter in a basin standing over a pan of hot water. Leave until melted, stirring once or twice. Gradually beat in 1 teaspoon vanilla essence (extract) and 8 oz. (just over $1\frac{1}{2}$ cups) sifted icing (confectioner's) sugar. If icing is too thin, add a little extra sifted sugar; if too thick, thin down with a few drops of water.

Devil's Food Cake

6 oz. ($1\frac{1}{2}$ cups) plain (all-purpose) flour
$\frac{1}{4}$ level teaspoon baking powder
$\frac{1}{4}$ level teaspoon bicarbonate of soda (baking soda)
2 oz. ($\frac{1}{4}$ cup) cocoa powder
4 oz. ($\frac{1}{2}$ cup) butter or margarine
10 oz. ($1\frac{1}{4}$ cups) castor (granulated) sugar
2 standard eggs
$\frac{1}{4}$ pint less 4 tablespoons (1 cup) water

Filling
$\frac{1}{4}$–$\frac{1}{2}$ pint (1 cup) double cream (whipping cream)

Icing and decoration
12 oz. (2 cups) icing (confectioner's) sugar
Warm water
Chocolate vermicelli

Pre-heat oven to moderate (350°F, Gas Mark 4). Well grease two 8 in. sandwich tins (pans) with melted fat. Line the bases with greased grease-proof (waxed) paper.

Sift together the flour, baking powder, soda and cocoa.

Cream the butter or margarine and sugar together until light and fluffy then beat in the whole eggs, one at a time, adding a dessertspoon (tablespoon) sifted dry ingredients with each. Using a metal spoon, fold in the remaining dry ingredients alternately with water.

When smooth and evenly combined, divide the mixture equally between the prepared tins (pans) and bake in the centre of the oven for about 50–60 minutes, or until risen and firm.

Leave in the tins (pans) for 5 minutes, then turn out on to a wire (cake) rack. Peel away the paper. When completely cold, sandwich the cakes and coat the sides with whipped cream.

To make the icing: sift the sugar into a bowl, then gradually mix to a *thick* icing with warm water, adding it teaspoon by teaspoon.

Spread over the top of the cake and leave until set. Decorate the sides and outer edge of cake top with chocolate vermicelli.

American frosted devil's food layer

American Frosted Devil's Food Layer

Make exactly as Devil's Food Cake (page 30). When cold, peel away paper and slice each cake horizontally.

To make chocolate butter cream filling: melt 2 oz. (2 squares) broken plain (bitter) chocolate in a bowl over hot water. Leave until almost cold but still liquid. Meanwhile, beat 2 oz. (¼ cup) butter with 3 oz. (½ cup) sifted icing (confectioner's) sugar until light and fluffy.

Gradually beat in cooled chocolate and 1 teaspoon vanilla essence (extract). Leave in a cool place until butter cream has firmed-up slightly then use to sandwich layers of cake together. To make American Frosting: put 1 lb. (2 cups) granulated sugar in a heavy pan with ¼ pint (⅝ cup) water. Stir over a low heat until the sugar dissolves. Bring to the boil and boil briskly, without stirring, until a little of the mixture forms a firm ball when dropped into cup of cold water, and the water itself remains clear (250°F on sugar thermometer). Remove from heat. Beat 2 egg whites to a *stiff* snow. Still beating with one hand, very gradually add the syrup in a slow, steady stream. Continue beating until the icing is cold and thick enough to spread. Swirl over the top and sides of the cake with a knife or back of a teaspoon and leave 3–4 hours in a cool place to set firmly.

Note : To flavour the Frosting, add 1 teaspoon vanilla, almond or rum essence (extract) to the syrup after removing from the heat.

Victoria sandwich cake (1) (above)
Chocolate layer loaf (below left) Coconut squares (below right)

Chocolate Nut Brownies

3 oz. (¾ cup) plain (all-purpose) flour
1½ oz. (4 T) cocoa powder
½ level teaspoon baking powder
4 oz. (½ cup) butter or margarine
8 oz. (1 cup) soft brown sugar
1 teaspoon vanilla essence (extract)
2 large eggs
2 oz. (½ cup) walnuts, chopped

Pre-heat oven to moderate (350°F, Gas Mark 4). Well grease and paper-line a 12 × 8 in. Swiss roll tin (jelly roll pan), and then grease the paper.
Sift together the flour, cocoa and baking powder. Cream the butter or margarine with the sugar and essence (extract) until light and fluffy, then beat in the whole eggs, one at a time, adding a dessertspoon (tablespoon) sifted dry ingredients with each. Stir in the walnuts then lightly fold in the remaining dry ingredients with a large metal spoon. Transfer to the prepared tin (pan) and bake in the centre of the oven for 30 minutes or until well-risen and golden.
Leave until lukewarm, cut into wide fingers, then turn onto a wire (cake) rack to cool. Store in an air-tight container when cold.

Butterscotch Walnut Brownies

4 oz. (½ cup) luxury or easy-cream (soft) margarine
4 oz. (½ cup) soft brown sugar
2 standard eggs
1 teaspoon vanilla essence (extract)
3 oz. (¾ cup) self-raising flour, sifted
2 oz. (½ cup) walnuts, chopped

Pre-heat oven to warm (325°F, Gas Mark 3). Brush a 7 in. square cake tin (pan) with melted fat. Line the base and sides with greaseproof (waxed) paper and brush with more fat.

Butterscotch walnut brownies

Place all the ingredients in a mixing bowl and beat together with a wooden spoon for 3–4 minutes or until thoroughly mixed.
Transfer to the prepared tin (pan) and bake in the centre of the oven for 35–45 minutes or until well risen and firm.
Leave in the tin (pan) for 5 minutes, then turn out onto a wire (cake) rack. Peel away paper. Cut into squares when completely cold.

Chocolate Fudge Cake

5 oz. (1¼ cups) self-raising flour
1 oz. (¼ cup) cocoa powder
6 oz. (¾ cup) butter
6 oz. (¾ cup) soft brown sugar
3 standard eggs, beaten
2 oz. (2 squares) plain (bitter) chocolate
1 teaspoon vanilla essence (extract)

Icing
2 oz. (¼ cup) butter
6 oz. (¾ cup) soft brown sugar (light in colour)
Finely grated peel and juice of 1 medium orange
1 oz. (1 square) plain (bitter) chocolate, chopped
6 oz. (just over 1 cup) icing (confectioner's) sugar

Decoration
2 oz. (2 squares) plain (bitter) chocolate

Pre-heat oven to moderate (350°F, Gas Mark 4). Brush an 8 in. round cake tin (pan) with melted fat. Line the base and sides with greaseproof (waxed) paper. Brush with more fat.
Sift together the flour and cocoa powder.
Cream the butter and sugar until light and fluffy. Beat in the whole eggs, one at a time, adding a dessertspoon sifted dry ingredients with each.
Place the chocolate in a small bowl and stand over a pan of hot water. Leave until melted. Cool, then beat into the creamed mixture with the vanilla essence (extract). Using a large metal spoon, fold in the remaining dry ingredients.
Transfer to the prepared tin (pan) and bake in the centre of the oven until well risen and firm, about 1–1¼ hours or until a cocktail stick etc. inserted into the centre comes out clean. Leave in the tin (pan) for 10 minutes then turn out and cool on a wire (cake) rack. Peel away paper.
To make icing: put butter, sugar, orange peel and juice into a saucepan. Heat together gently, stirring, until the sugar dissolves. Remove from the heat, add the chocolate and stir until melted. Gradually stir in the icing (confectioner's) sugar, then beat until smooth and easily spread.

Split the cake in half and fill with a little icing. Spread the rest over the top then, using a round-bladed knife, make a pattern on it.

To decorate: put the chocolate into a strong polythene bag, tie a knot in the top and place in a bowl of hot water. When the chocolate has melted, snip off one bottom corner of the bag and trickle the chocolate in a zig-zag pattern over the top of the cake.

Mocha Fudge Cake

Make exactly as Chocolate Fudge Cake (above). When cold, split in half and sandwich together with chocolate spread.

To make Fudge Frosting: Put 2 oz. ($\frac{1}{4}$ cup) butter or margarine in a saucepan with 4 oz. ($\frac{1}{2}$ cup) soft brown sugar, 3 tablespoons ($3\frac{3}{4}$ T) liquid coffee essence (strong coffee) and 1 tablespoon ($1\frac{1}{4}$ T) undiluted evaporated milk. Dissolve over a low heat, stirring. Bring to the boil then boil briskly for 3 minutes only. Remove from the heat and gradually beat in 1 lb. (about $3\frac{1}{2}$ cups) sifted icing (confectioner's) sugar. Continue beating until the frosting is cold and beginning to thicken, then quickly spread over the top and sides of cake.

To decorate: put 2 oz. (2 squares) plain (bitter) chocolate in a strong polythene bag, tie the top in a knot and place in a bowl of hot water.

When chocolate has melted, snip off one bottom corner and pipe a zig-zag border round the edge of the cake and circles in the centre. Leave until set before cutting.

Mushroom Cake

3 oz. (3 squares) plain (bitter) chocolate, broken up
2 tablespoons ($2\frac{1}{2}$ T) milk
5 oz. ($1\frac{1}{4}$ cups) self-raising flour
Dash of salt
4 oz. ($\frac{1}{2}$ cup) butter or margarine
4 oz. ($\frac{1}{2}$ cup) castor (granulated) sugar
2 standard eggs
Almond Paste
4 oz. ($\frac{1}{2}$ cup) ground almonds
2 oz. (3 T) icing (confectioner's) sugar, sifted
2 level tablespoons ($2\frac{1}{2}$ T) castor (granulated) sugar
Squeeze of lemon juice
1 egg yolk
1 tablespoon warmed apricot jam (preserves), sieved
Cream Topping
2 oz. ($\frac{1}{4}$ cup) butter
4 oz. ($\frac{3}{4}$ cup) icing (confectioner's) sugar, sifted

Chocolate fudge cake

1 oz. (1 square) plain (bitter) chocolate, dissolved in 2 teaspoons hot milk

Pre-heat oven to moderately hot (375°F, Gas Mark 5). Well grease an 8-in. deep sandwich tin (layer cake pan) and line the base with greaseproof (waxed) paper.

Break up the chocolate and put in a pan with the milk. Leave over a low heat until the chocolate melts. Cool.

Sift together the flour and salt.

Cream the butter or margarine with the sugar until light and fluffy then beat in the whole eggs, one at a time, adding a dessertspoon (tablespoon) sifted flour with each. Add the chocolate/milk mixture and a further spoon of flour and beat well. Using a metal spoon, gently fold in remaining flour.

Transfer to the prepared tin (pan) and bake in the centre of the oven for approximately 30–40 minutes or until well risen and firm. Turn onto a wire cooling (cake) rack, peel away the paper and leave until completely cold.

To make almond paste: mix the almonds and both sugars and bind with the lemon juice and egg yolk. Turn on to sugared surface. Knead and roll out into a 10 in. circle. Brush with jam (preserves) and place the cake in the centre. Press the almond paste against the sides of the cake and trim away the excess from the top edges. Roll the trimmings to form a 'stalk'.

To make the cream topping: cream together the butter and sugar then gradually beat in melted chocolate. Beat well and leave in the cool until the cream firms up. Pipe or spread on top of the cake, marking grooves with a fork to resemble a mushroom. Place 'stalk' in centre.

Chocolate frosted loaf (left)
Devil's food cake (right)
Mushroom cake (below)

Sand Cake

4 oz. (1 cup) plain (all-purpose) flour
4 oz. (1 cup) cornflour (cornstarch)
$\frac{1}{4}$ level teaspoon salt
2 level teaspoons baking powder
6 oz. ($\frac{3}{4}$ cup) butter or margarine
6 oz. ($\frac{3}{4}$ cup) castor (granulated) sugar
Finely grated peel of 1 small lemon
3 standard eggs
3 tablespoons ($3\frac{3}{4}$ T) cold milk

Pre-heat oven to moderate (350°F, Gas Mark 4). Brush a 7 in. round cake tin (pan) with melted fat. Line the base and sides with greaseproof (waxed) paper. Brush the paper with more fat. Sift together the flour, cornflour (cornstarch), salt and baking powder. Cream the butter or margarine, sugar and lemon peel until light and fluffy, then beat in the whole eggs, one at a time, adding a tablespoon sifted dry ingredients with each. Using a large metal spoon, fold in the remaining dry ingredients alternately with the milk.

Transfer the mixture to the prepared tin (pan) and bake in the centre of the oven for $1\frac{1}{4}$–$1\frac{1}{2}$ hours until well risen and golden, or until cocktail stick etc. inserted into the centre comes out clean.

Leave in the tin (pan) for about 10 minutes, then turn out onto a wire (cake) rack. Carefully peel away the paper. Store in an air-tight container when cold.

Chocolate Ginger Gateau

6 oz. ($1\frac{1}{2}$ cups) self-raising flour
Dash of salt
4 level teaspoons powdered ginger
6 oz. ($\frac{3}{4}$ cup) butter or margarine
5 oz. (10 T) soft brown sugar
3 standard eggs

Filling
6 tablespoons ($7\frac{1}{2}$ T) double cream (whipping cream)

Chocolate icing
3 oz. (3 squares) plain (bitter) chocolate, broken into small pieces
$1\frac{1}{2}$ tablespoons ($1\frac{5}{8}$ T) water
2 teaspoons softened butter
8 oz. ($1\frac{1}{2}$ cups) icing (confectioner's) sugar, sifted
1 teaspoon vanilla essence (extract)

Decoration
2 oz. crystallized ginger cut into pieces

Pre-heat oven to moderate (350°F, Gas Mark 4). Well grease two 8 in. sandwich tins (layer cake pans) and line the bases with greased greaseproof (waxed) paper.
Sift together the flour, salt and ginger.
Cream the butter or margarine and sugar together until light and fluffy, then beat in the whole eggs, one at a time, adding a dessertspoon (tablespoon) sifted dry ingredients with each. Using a large metal spoon, gently fold in remaining dry ingredients.
Divide equally between the prepared tins (pans) and bake in the centre of the oven for 20–30 minutes or until well risen and firm.
Leave in the tins (pans) for 5 minutes then turn on to a wire (cake) rack.
When completely cold, peel away the paper and sandwich together with cream, whipped until thick.
To make icing: put the chocolate, water and butter into a bowl standing over a pan of hot water. Leave until melted, stirring once or twice. Gradually beat in the icing (confectioner's) sugar and continue beating until icing is smooth and shiny, then stir in the vanilla essence (extract).
Pour the icing over the top of the cake, allowing it to run down the sides. Smooth with a round-bladed knife (spatula) dipped in hot water, leave icing to set slightly then decorate edge with pieces of ginger.

Apple Layer Cake

Make up Victoria Sandwich mixture (see page 24) using 6 oz. ($1\frac{1}{2}$ cups) self-raising flour, dash of salt, 6 oz. ($\frac{3}{4}$ cup) butter or margarine, 6 oz. ($\frac{3}{4}$ cup) castor (granulated) sugar and 3 standard eggs.
Transfer mixture to a well greased, paper-lined 7 in. loose-bottomed (spring-form) cake tin (pan).

Apple layer cake

Topping
2 level tablespoons ($2\frac{1}{2}$ T) plain (all-
  purpose) flour
1 level teaspoon cinnamon
1 level tablespoon ($1\frac{1}{4}$ T) castor (granulated) sugar
1 oz. (2 T) butter or margarine, melted

Sift the flour and cinnamon together. Add the
sugar and melted butter or margarine. Stir with a
fork until fine crumbs are formed then sprinkle
over the top of the cake.
Bake in the centre of a moderate oven (350°F,
Gas Mark 4) for 1 hour or until well risen and
firm, or until a cocktail stick etc. inserted into
the centre comes out clean.
Leave for 5 minutes then carefully remove from
the tin (pan). Cool on a wire (cake) rack until
completely cold then slice horizontally in two
layers.

Apple filling
1 breakfast cup (1 cup) thick apple sauce
1 egg yolk
1 level tablespoon ($1\frac{1}{4}$ T) icing (confectioner's) sugar

Pour all the ingredients into a pan. Heat, without boiling, until very thick. Leave until cold.
Use to sandwich cake together before serving.

Ginger Fruit Cake

8 oz. (2 cups) self-raising flour
$\frac{1}{2}$ level teaspoon salt
2 level teaspoons ground ginger
1 level teaspoon cinnamon or mixed spice
4 oz. ($\frac{1}{2}$ cup) butter
4 oz. ($\frac{1}{2}$ cup) castor (granulated) sugar
1 large egg, beaten
2 level tablespoons ($2\frac{1}{2}$ T) black treacle
  (molasses)
$\frac{1}{4}$ level teaspoon bicarbonate of soda
  (baking soda)
9 fl. oz. ($1\frac{1}{8}$ cups) buttermilk
6 oz. (just over 1 cup) sultanas or seedless
  raisins

Pre-heat oven to moderate (350°F, Gas Mark 4).
Well grease a $11 \times 7 \times 1\frac{1}{2}$ in. tin (pan). Line the
base and sides with greased greaseproof (waxed)
paper.
Sift together the flour, salt and spices.
Cream the butter and sugar together until light
and fluffy then beat in the egg and treacle. Stir
in a quarter of the flour mixture. Mix the soda in
the buttermilk, then stir a little of it into the cake
mixture. Add the fruit, remaining flour mixture
and remaining liquid. Mix well, and turn into
the prepared tin (pan).
Spread level with a knife and bake in the centre
of the oven for about 45 minutes. Leave in the
tin (pan) for 10 minutes then turn out and cool on
a wire (cake) rack. Peel away the paper and leave
until completely cold before cutting into fingers.
Store in an air-tight container.

Ginger fruit cake

Chocolate marzipan ripples (top left)
Battenburg cake (top right)
Mocha fudge cake (below)

Spice Ring

10 oz. (2½ cups) plain (all-purpose) flour
1 level teaspoon bicarbonate of soda
  (baking soda)
½ level teaspoon cinnamon and mixed
  spice
4 oz. (½ cup) butter or margarine
6 oz. (¾ cup) castor (granulated) sugar
2 standard eggs
8 level tablespoons (10 T) raspberry or
  apricot jam (preserves)
4 tablespoons (5 T) hot water

Pre-heat oven to warm (325°F, Gas Mark 3).
Well grease a 7 in. fluted ring tin (mould).
Sift together the flour, soda, and spices.
Cream the butter or margarine with the sugar
until light and fluffy then beat in the whole eggs,
one at a time, adding a dessertspoon (tablespoon)
sifted dry ingredients with each. Beat in the jam
(preserves) then fold in the remaining dry
ingredients alternately with water.
Transfer to the prepared tin (mould) and bake in
the centre of the oven for about 1 hour or until
the cake is well risen and firm. Turn out on to a
wire (cake) rack and leave until completely cold.
To ice cake: mix 6 oz. (1 cup) icing (confectioner's) sugar to a smooth icing with strained orange
juice, adding it teaspoon by teaspoon.

Chocolate Cream
Leaf Gateau

Make up either Victoria Sandwich Cake or
Chocolate Sandwich Cake (see pages 24 and 25).
When completely cold, peel away paper.

Chocolate Butter Cream
6 oz. (¾ cup) butter, softened
12 oz. (2 cups) icing (confectioner's) sugar,
  sifted
1 tablespoon (1¼ T) milk
3 oz. (3 squares) melted and cooled dark
  (bitter) chocolate
A little cocoa powder

Beat butter until very soft. Gradually beat in the
icing sugar alternately with the milk and melted
chocolate. Continue beating until the mixture is
light and creamy. Leave in a cool place for a
short time to firm-up. Use a little to fill the cake.
Cover the top and sides with more butter cream,
leaving a little on one side.
Ridge the top and sides of the cake with a large-
pronged fork. Darken the remaining butter
cream by beating in a little sifted cocoa and a
few drops of milk if it becomes too thick.
Transfer the cake to a platter and, with the
darkened butter cream, pipe lines of rosettes
or shells round the top and lower edges.
To make leaves: break chocolate on to a plate
standing over pan of hot water and leave until
melted. Wash and dry a handful of rose or other
small leaves and draw each, ribbed side downwards, over melted chocolate. Leave to dry on

Chocolate cream leaf gateau
*1 : Leaves being drawn over melted chocolate and
then stood on foil   2 : Finished cake*

42

piece of foil. When firm but still pliable, carefully peel off chocolate 'leaves'. Store in a cool, dry place and use as required.

To complete cake: arrange a cluster of leaves on top and fill in the centre with halved glacé cherries.

Chocolate Marzipan Ripples

4 oz. (1 cup) self-raising flour
Dash of salt
4 oz. (½ cup) butter or margarine
4 oz. (½ cup) castor (granulated) sugar
2 standard eggs
4 level tablespoons (5 T) apricot jam (preserves)
8 oz. bought or home-made marzipan
Red and green food colourings
Cocoa powder
8 oz. (8 squares) plain (semi-sweet) chocolate
1 oz. (2 T) butter
3 tablespoons (3¾ T) water
2 heaped tablespoons (¼ cup) icing (confectioner's) sugar, sifted

Pre-heat oven to moderate (350°F, Gas Mark 4). Brush a 7 in. square cake tin (pan) with melted fat. Line the base and sides with greaseproof (waxed) paper and brush paper with more fat. Sift together the flour and salt.

Cream the butter or margarine and sugar together until light and fluffy, then beat in the whole eggs, one at a time, adding a dessertspoon (tablespoon) sifted flour with each. Using a metal spoon, gently fold in the remaining flour. Transfer to the prepared tin (pan) and bake in the centre of the oven for 35–45 minutes until well risen and firm, or until a cocktail stick etc. inserted into the centre comes out clean. Leave in the tin (pan) for 10 minutes then turn out and cool on a wire (cake) rack. Peel away the paper. Cut the cake in half horizontally when completely cold. Sandwich together with jam (preserves) and cut off brown edges. Cut the cake into two strips. Brush the top and sides with the remaining jam.

Divide the marzipan in three equal pieces; work green colouring into one piece, red colouring into the second and cocoa powder into the third. Divide each piece of coloured marzipan in two and form into 7 in. long rolls. Place three different coloured rolls on both pieces of cake, forming a triangle. Transfer to a wire (cake) rack.

To make chocolate coating: break up the chocolate and put with butter and water in a bowl over

Glacé fruit cake

a pan of hot water. Leave until melted, then beat in the icing (confectioner's) sugar. Spoon over the cakes, smoothing the sides with a flat-bladed knife. Make sure the chocolate coating is even by shaking the rack gently. When set, cut each cake into 6 diagonal slices.

Glacé Fruit Cake

9 oz. (2¼ cups) self-raising flour
1 oz. (3 T) cornflour (cornstarch)
8 oz. (1 cup) butter
8 oz. (1 cup) castor (granulated) sugar
4 standard eggs
2 tablespoons (2½ T) glacé cherries, quartered
1 tablespoon (1¼ T) chopped angelica
1½ oz. (¼ cup) crystallized orange slices, chopped
1½ oz. (¼ cup) crystallized pineapple, chopped
1 level tablespoon (1¼ T) blanched and chopped pistachio nuts or almonds
Finely grated peel and juice of ½ a medium lemon

Frosting
American Frosting (see page 32)

Decoration
2 slices glacé orange
Glacé cherries
Angelica

Pre-heat oven to warm (325°F, Gas Mark 3). Brush a 7 in. round cake tin (pan) with melted fat. Line the base and sides with greaseproof (waxed) paper then brush paper with more fat. Sift together the flour and cornflour (cornstarch).

Cream the butter and sugar together until light and fluffy, then beat in the whole eggs, one at a

time, adding a dessertspoon (tablespoon) dry ingredients with each. Stir in the prepared glacé fruits, nuts and lemon peel and juice. Using a metal spoon, fold in the remaining dry ingredients. When evenly combined, transfer to the prepared tin (pan) and bake in the centre of the oven for 1¼–1½ hours until well risen and golden, or until cocktail stick etc. inserted into the centre comes out clean.

Leave in the tin (pan) for 5 minutes, then turn out and cool on wire (cake) rack. Peel away the paper when completely cold, pour the American Frosting quickly over the whole cake and swirl with a knife. Leave 2–3 hours to set, then decorate with pieces of glacé orange, cherries and angelica.

Mandarin Mocha Cake

Make up Victoria Sandwich Cake mixture (see page 24), making double quantity.

Transfer to two greased and paper-lined 12 × 8 × 1½ in. Swiss roll tins (jelly roll pans). Bake in the centre of a moderate oven (350°F, Gas Mark 4) for 20–25 minutes or until well-risen and firm. Leave in the tins (pans) for 5 minutes, then turn out on to wire (cake) racks. When cold, peel away paper.

Trim away crusty edges with a sharp knife, then cut each cake into two 6 × 8 in. strips. Beat 6 oz. (¾ cup) softened butter with 12 oz. (just under 2½ cups) sifted icing (confectioners') sugar and 2 tablespoons (2½ T) liquid coffee essence (strong coffee). Divide this butter cream into two portions. Drain 2 cans of mandarin oranges. Reserve about 24 segments for decoration, chop remainder and stir into one portion of the butter cream with 3 oz. (¾ cup) finely chopped walnuts. Sandwich the cake together with the mandarin/nut butter cream.

Spread the second portion of butter cream over the top and sides of the cake. Decorate with the reserved mandarin segments and walnut halves. Chill lightly before cutting and serving.

Note : Reserve syrup from cans of mandarins and use as a base for jelly, etc.

Battenburg Cake

Make up Victoria Sandwich Cake mixture as directed in recipe (see page 24), but use double quantity of ingredients.

Divide the mixture in half and gently fold sufficient red colouring into one portion to make it a fairly deep pink.

Grease and line a 12 × 8 × 1½ in. Swiss roll tin (jelly roll pan), making sure the paper protrudes about 1 in. above the top edge of the tin. Divide

the tin in half lengthwise by standing a wide band of cardboard, wrapped in foil, down centre to form a wall. Put pink mixture in one half and plain mixture in the other.

Bake in the centre of a moderate oven (350°F, Gas Mark 4) for about 35–45 minutes until well risen and firm. Remove from the oven, leave in the tin (pan) for 5 minutes then turn both pieces out to cool on a wire (cake) rack.

When cold, trim both pieces of cake to the same size (this is easily done by standing one piece of cake on top of the other and trimming the edges with a sharp knife), then cut each piece of cake lengthwise (4 pieces). Spread the lengths of cake all over with melted apricot jam (preserves), then form into a block, alternating the colours as shown in the photograph, page 41. Brush again with jam (preserves), then wrap in 8 oz. (1 cup) almond paste rolled approximately 8 × 10 in. Press the almond paste well on to the cake, making sure the join is well sealed. Pinch up the edges between finger and thumb to give a crimped effect. Criss-cross the top with a sharp knife, or decorate with half a glacé cherry and 2 pieces of angelica. Cut a thin slice off both ends for added neatness.

Hazelnut Coffee Gateau

Make up Victoria Sandwich Cake in two 7 in. tins (pans) as directed in recipe (see page 24).

When cold, sandwich together and coat top and sides with Coffee Butter Cream: beat 6 oz. (¾ cup) butter until soft, then gradually beat in 12 oz. (just under 2½ cups) sifted icing (confectioners') sugar and 2 tablespoons (2½ T) liquid coffee essence (strong coffee).

Press 2 oz. (½ cup) chopped hazelnuts against sides of cake. Put remaining butter cream into an icing (pastry) bag fitted with a star-shaped tube and pipe scrolls round top edge and centre of the cake. Decorate with whole walnuts.

Hazelnut coffee gateau

Walnut spice sandwich

Strawberry cream and almond ring

Strawberry Cream and Almond Ring

Victoria Sandwich mixture (see page 24)
2 tablespoons (2½ T) sweet sherry
1 tablespoon (1¼ T) orange squash (soda)
½ pint (1¼ cups) double cream (whipping cream)
2 tablespoons (2½ T) milk
1 heaped tablespoon (2 T) icing (confectioners') sugar, sifted
1 lb. (approximately 2½ cups) strawberries, washed and hulled
1 tablespoon (1¼ T) almonds, blanched, split and toasted

Pre-heat oven to moderately hot (375°F, Gas Mark 5). Well grease a 9 in. ring tin (pan).
Place the Victoria Sandwich mixture in the prepared tin (pan) and bake in the centre of the oven for 30–35 minutes or until well-risen and firm to the touch. Leave in the tin (pan) for 10 minutes, then turn out on to a wire (cake) rack. When cold, transfer to a serving plate.
Mix together the sherry and orange squash (soda) and pour over the cake, letting it soak in. Whip the cream and milk until stiff, then stir in the icing (confectioners') sugar. Place a quarter of the whipped cream in a forcing (pastry) bag fitted with a star-shaped tube. Spread the remaining cream over the cake, covering it completely.
Pile all but 6 of the strawberries in the centre. Decorate the sides of the ring with piped cream, remaining halved strawberries and almonds.

Rich Shortbread

4 oz. (½ cup) butter, softened
2 oz. (¼ cup) castor (granulated) sugar
2 oz. (½ cup) cornflour (cornstarch)
4 oz. (1 cup) plain (all-purpose) flour

Pre-heat oven to warm, (325°F, Gas Mark 3). Cream the butter, sugar and cornflour (cornstarch) until light and creamy. Work in the flour and knead lightly to form a soft, smooth dough. Press into an 8 in. fluted flan ring standing on an ungreased baking tray (sheet), or roll into an 8 in. circle about ½ in. thick and cut with a large shortbread cutter. Prick lightly with a fork and mark into 8 sections with a sharp knife.
Bake in the centre of the oven for 35–40 minutes or until pale biscuit colour. Sprinkle with castor (granulated) sugar and serve cut into sections.

Assorted light cakes

These cakes are nearly always fatless (with a few exceptions such as Genoese Sponge and Sandwich Cake made with oil). They are therefore light and spongy with a soft, tender texture that gives them a unique and distinctive delicacy. Swiss rolls (jelly rolls), the traditional nursery tea Sponge Sandwich, and an assortment of sumptuous gateaux and torte can all be made, quite easily, from a basic mixture of sugar, eggs and flour; Chiffon Cake, which is as soft and floating as its name suggests, is also included in this repertoire.

Many of these cakes depend for their lightness on air, as opposed to chemical raising agents such as baking powder, and the air is incorporated into the mixture by whisking together eggs and sugar until they treble in volume and become thick, very pale in colour and foamy. By hand, this can be a slow and laborious task, but standing the mixing bowl over hot water and using a balloon whisk helps to speed things up. So does a cake mixer – they make these cakes quicker than any other.

The usual proportions are easy to remember because the basic ingredients for a 7 in. sponge sandwich are 3 of everything: 3 oz. flour ($\frac{3}{4}$ cup all-purpose flour), 3 oz. (6 T) castor (granulated) sugar and 3 standard eggs. For Sandwich Cakes and Swiss rolls (jelly rolls) one can get away with using self-raising flour instead of plain (all-purpose), but when the same mixture is transferred to a deep tin, plain (all-purpose) flour is essential otherwise the cakes will rise too much initially and then fall dramatically in the middle.

I must also add another point about flour: for good results, the flour should be sifted twice or even three times before being cut and folded into the mixture. Cutting and folding flour into a mixture really needs to be demonstrated, but in simple terms the flour is sprinkled on to the whisked ingredients, the edge of a metal spoon is then drawn across the mixture (the spoon should touch the base of the bowl) and then flicked over with a quick turn of the wrist. This is repeated until all the flour has been thoroughly incorporated. A light hand, or hand movement, is more important at this stage than speed, and the cutting and folding operation may be carried out virtually in slow motion, as long as stirring or beating is avoided.

Tin (pan) preparation is another thing which requires care. Many people simply flour the tins (pans) while others brush them lightly with melted fat or oil; I, erring on the cautious side, brush all tins (pans) lightly with oil or melted margarine, line the base and sides with greaseproof (waxed) paper and brush the paper again with a thin layer of oil or melted margarine. Sponge mixtures, like soufflés, drop if the oven door is opened while the cakes are rising and it makes good sense to leave the oven door tightly closed until the cakes are cooked or almost cooked. Those without glass-fronted, see-through oven doors have no choice but to curb their curiosity!

Finally, as with all other cakes, the ingredients should be at room temperature, and when the cakes themselves are turned out of the tins (pans), they should be done so on a tea-towel resting on a wire cooling (cake) rack. If turned directly on to racks, the wires would cut into the surfaces.

Some common faults

Texture biscuity and close

1. Insufficient whisking of eggs and sugar.
2. Flour stirred into whisked eggs and sugar instead of being cut and folded in with a metal spoon.

Texture tacky and heavy
1. Too much sugar used.
2. Insufficient baking time allowed.
3. Oven too hot or too cool.

Deep sponge sunk in centre
1. Self-raising flour used instead of plain (all-purpose).
2. Oven too hot or too cool.
3. Insufficient baking time allowed.
4. Oven door opened while cake was rising.

Swiss (jelly) roll cracks
1. Over-cooked.
2. Texture biscuity and close (see above for reasons why).
3. Left to stand too long before being rolled.

Sponge Sandwich

3 oz. (¾ cup) plain (all-purpose) or self-raising flour
Dash of salt
3 standard eggs
3 oz. (6 T) castor (granulated) sugar

Pre-heat oven to moderate (350°F, Gas Mark 4). Brush two 7-in. sandwich tins (layer cake pans) with melted margarine or oil. Line the base and sides with greaseproof (waxed) paper. Brush the paper with more margarine or oil. Sift the flour and salt two or three times on to a plate or piece of greaseproof (waxed) paper.

Put the eggs into a bowl standing over a pan of hot water and beat with a balloon whisk until thickish and pale lemon coloured. Add the sugar and continue whisking until the mixture trebles in volume, is much paler and becomes thick and the consistency of softly whipped cream, about 10 minutes by hand or 5 minutes with a mixer. Sprinkle the flour over the top and gently and lightly cut and fold into the whisked eggs and sugar with a metal spoon.

When evenly combined, transfer to the prepared tins (pans) and bake in the centre of the oven 15–20 minutes or until well risen and golden. Turn out on to a towel-covered wire (cake) rack and peel away the paper. When completely cold, sandwich together with jam (preserves) and dust with castor (granulated) sugar.

Note: Raspberry jam (preserves) is the traditional jam to use for this particular cake.

Cream-filled Sponge Sandwich
If liked, sponges may be sandwiched together with whipped cream and jam (preserves) or whipped cream into which some well-drained canned and chopped fruit has been added.

Opposite top, Cream-filled sponge sandwich (behind left), Genoese iced squares (behind right) and Magic Circle (front)

Opposite below, Raspberry cream slice. Above, Sponge sandwich

1 : *Ingredients and tins (pans) already prepared*
3 : *Liquids being stirred into dry ingredients*

2 : *Liquids being lightly mixed together*
4 : *Egg whites being folded into batter with metal spoon*

Velvet sponge

Velvet Sponge

5 oz. (1¼ cups) plain (all-purpose) flour
1 oz. (¼ cup) cornflour (cornstarch)
2 level teaspoons baking powder
½ level teaspoon salt
5 oz. (10 T) castor (granulated) sugar
2 standard eggs
3½ fl. oz. (9 T) corn oil
3½ fl. oz. (7 T) water

Pre-heat oven to moderately hot (375°F, Gas Mark 5). Well grease and paper-line two 7 in. sandwich tins (layer cake pans). Grease the paper again. Sift the dry ingredients into a bowl. Separate the eggs. Add the yolks to the oil and water and mix lightly together with a fork. Stir into the dry ingredients to form a smooth, slack batter. Whisk the egg whites to a stiff snow and, using a metal spoon, fold into batter mixture. Transfer to the prepared tins (pans) and bake in the centre of the oven for 25–30 minutes or until well risen and golden. Allow to cool in the tins (pans) slightly before turning out onto a wire (cake) rack. Peel away the paper then sandwich together with jam (preserves). If liked, dust with castor (granulated) or sifted icing (confectioners') sugar.

Deep Sponge

Make Sponge Sandwich mixture as page 49, using *plain (all-purpose)* flour.
Transfer to a greased and paper-lined 7 in. cake tin (pan). Bake in the centre of warm oven (325°F, Gas Mark 3) for about 45 minutes until well risen and golden, or until a cocktail stick etc. inserted into the centre comes out clean. Leave in the tin (pan) for 5 minutes before turning out on a towel-covered wire (cake) rack. When completely cold, gently peel away the paper and cut the cake into three horizontal layers. Fill as desired with jam (preserves), lemon curd, sweetened whipped cream or butter cream.

Swiss (Jelly) Roll

Make up Sponge Sandwich mixture as page 49. Transfer to a greased and paper-lined 12 × 8 in. Swiss roll tin (jelly roll pan) and bake in the centre of a moderately hot oven (400°F, Gas Mark 6) for 10–12 minutes or until well-risen and golden.

Swiss (jelly) roll

Turn out on to large sheet of greaseproof (waxed) paper – first sprinkled with sugar – standing on folded damp towel or tea towel. Peel away the paper then quickly cut off the crusty edges.

Spread the cake quickly with about 4 table-spoons (5 T) jam (preserves) or lemon curd and roll up tightly. Hold in place for 1–2 minutes so that the roll does not uncurl.

Chocolate Swiss (Jelly) Roll

Make Sponge Sandwich mixture as page 49, substituting 1 level tablespoon ($1\frac{1}{4}$ T) cocoa powder for 1 level tablespoon ($1\frac{1}{4}$ T) flour. Then continue as directed for Swiss (jelly) roll.

Cream-filled Chocolate Swiss (Jelly) Roll

Follow recipe for Chocolate Swiss (Jelly) Roll (above), but after cutting off crusty edges, roll up Swiss (jelly) roll loosely with paper inside to prevent cake sticking to itself. Cover with a damp cloth and leave until cold.

Unroll, remove paper and fill with $\frac{1}{4}$ pint (1 cup) whipped cream (whipping cream), lightly sweetened with sifted icing (confectioners') sugar. Roll up again and hold in position for 1–2 minutes.

Chocolate Cake Surprise

Make up Sponge Sandwich mixture (see page 49), using 5 oz. ($1\frac{1}{4}$ cups) plain (all-purpose) flour sifted with 1 level teaspoon baking powder, 5 oz. (10 T) castor (granulated) sugar and 5 standard eggs.

Transfer just over half the mixture to a 14×10 in. greased, paper-lined Swiss roll tin (jelly roll pan). Bake in the centre of a moderately hot oven (400°F, Gas Mark 6) for 10–15 minutes or until well risen and firm. Turn out on to a towel-covered wire (cake) rack, peel away the paper then cover with a damp cloth.

Into the remaining mixture, gently cut and fold 3 level teaspoons sifted cocoa powder and 1 tea-spoon vanilla essence (extract). Transfer to a greased and paper-lined 8 in. round, deep sandwich tin (pan). Bake just below the mixture in the Swiss roll tin (jelly roll pan), allowing 10–15 minutes longer baking time, a total of 25–30 minutes. Turn out on to a towel-covered wire (cake) rack and peel away the paper.

While both cakes are cooking, make up Chocolate

1 : *Swiss (jelly) roll being cut into strips*
2 : *Spiral being formed on top of cake*

Butter Cream: Beat 8 oz. (1 cup) butter until soft. Gradually beat in 12 oz. (2½ cups) sifted icing (confectioners') sugar. Continue beating until light and fluffy. Reserve 1 heaped tablespoon (1¼ T) for decorating the top of the cake. Combine 3 level tablespoons (3¾ T) cocoa powder with sufficient boiling water to form a thickish paste. Leave until almost cold, then gradually beat into the butter cream.

To make up cake: Cut the Swiss (jelly) roll lengthwise into 5 even strips (see first picture). Split the chocolate cake horizontally in half and spread the cut surfaces with chocolate butter cream. Spread the strips of cake with more butter cream and form each into a roll, placing on top of half the chocolate sandwich as you do so (see second picture). Use all the strips in the same way, so that the cut of half the cake is completely covered with a spiral.

Place the second cake on top then cover all over with the remaining chocolate butter cream. Press chocolate vermicelli or grated chocolate against the sides of the cake then transfer to a plate. If the plain butter cream has hardened, beat until soft with 1–2 teaspoons warm water. Pipe straight lines – 1 in. apart – on top of the cake. Make a 'feather' pattern by drawing a skewer in alternate directions across the lines.

Lemon Hazelnut Torte

Make a Deep Sponge (see page 50), gently folding in 1 oz. (¼ cup) finely ground hazelnuts

and 1 level teaspoon grated lemon peel before cutting and folding in the sifted flour.

When cold, slice into 3 layers. Fill and coat the top and sides with Lemon Butter Cream, made by creaming 8 oz. (1 cup) butter with 12 oz. (just under 2½ cups) sifted icing (confectioners') sugar until light and fluffy. Beat in 3–4 teaspoons lemon juice and 1 level teaspoon finely grated lemon peel.

Press coarsely chopped hazelnuts against the sides then transfer the cake to a plate. Using the remaining butter cream, pipe large rosettes round the top edge, then decorate the top with segments of sugar-coated lemon jelly slices.

Coffee Almond Torte

Make a Sponge Sandwich (see page 49).
Whip ½ pint (1¼ cups) double cream (whipping cream) with 1 tablespoon (1¼ T) *very strong coffee* and sifted icing (confectioners') sugar to taste.

Sandwich the cake together with some of the cream, spread some more over top and sides. Press flaked almonds against the sides then transfer Torte to a plate. Ridge the top of the cake in circular lines with a fork then, using remaining cream, pipe 8 rosettes on the outer edge and one in the centre.

Walnut Cream Torte

Make a Deep Sponge (see page 50), gently folding in 1 oz. (¼ cup) finely ground walnuts and 1 teaspoon vanilla essence (extract) before folding in the flour.

When cold, slice horizontally into 3 layers and sandwich together with apricot jam (preserves). Whip ½ pint (1¼ cups) double cream (whipping cream) until softly stiff. Add vanilla essence (extract) and icing (confectioners') sugar to taste. Transfer the cake to a plate and cover the top and sides with the whipped cream, swirling it on with a knife. Stud the sides with walnut halves and chill lightly before serving.
To economize: mock cream may be used if preferred.

Walnut Spice Sandwich

Make a Sponge Sandwich (see page 49), sifting the flour with 1 level teaspoon mixed spice or cinnamon and gently folding in 1 oz. (¼ cup) chopped walnuts to whisked eggs and sugar before cutting and folding in dry ingredients.

When completely cold, sandwich together with whipped cream or butter cream and arrange walnut halves attractively on top.

Coffee almond torte (front)
and Walnut cream torte (behind)

Frosted fruit sandwich

Peanut butter frosted layer

Frosted Fruit Sandwich

Make a Sponge Sandwich (see page 49).
When cold, sandwich together with black-currant jam (preserves). Cover the top and sides with half quantity of American Frosting (see page 32) and leave 2–3 hours to set.

Raspberry Cream Slice

Make up Sponge Sandwich mixture (see page 49) and bake as a Swiss roll (jelly roll) (page 50). When cold, trim the edges and cut the cake in half lengthwise. Sandwich together with $\frac{1}{4}$ pint ($\frac{5}{8}$ cup) sweetened whipped cream and fresh raspberries. Cover the top with more raspberries. Using remaining cream, pipe 2 heavy lines down either side of the slice. Chill lightly before serving.

Economical Fruit Cream Slice: Instead of fresh fruit, use 1 can raspberry or cherry pie filling.

Peanut Butter Frosted Layer

Make up Sponge Sandwich mixture (see page 49) and bake as a Swiss roll (jelly roll).
When cold, trim the edges and cut the cake lengthwise into 3 equal strips.

To make Peanut Butter Frosting: cream 4 oz. ($\frac{1}{2}$ cup) peanut butter with 3 oz. (6 T) butter or margarine and 10 oz. ($1\frac{1}{2}$ cups) sifted icing (confectioners') sugar. Beat in 1 tablespoon ($1\frac{1}{4}$ T) liquid coffee essence (strong coffee) and 1 tablespoon ($1\frac{1}{4}$ T) milk.

Sandwich the cake together with some of the frosting, spread remainder over the top and sides. Transfer to a plate and arrange a line of halved and seeded black grapes along the centre.

Magic Circle

Make up Sponge Sandwich mixture (see page 49) using plain (all-purpose) flour and transfer to an 8 in. well greased ring tin (mould).
Bake in the centre of a warm oven (325°F, Gas Mark 3) for about 35–45 minutes or until well-risen and firm.
Turn out on to a towel-covered wire (cake) rack and leave until completely cold. Remove the towel and return the cake to the rack.
To make Chocolate Frosting: melt 3 oz. (3 squares) broken plain (semi-sweet) chocolate, 1 teaspoon butter and 1 tablespoon ($1\frac{1}{4}$ T) strong coffee in a bowl standing over a pan of hot water. Stir in 3 oz. ($\frac{1}{2}$ cup) sifted icing (confectioners') sugar.

Pour over the cake, allowing it to trickle down the sides. When almost set, sprinkle the top with chopped walnuts.

Genoese Sandwich

2 oz. ($\frac{1}{4}$ cup) butter
3 large eggs
3 oz. (4 T) castor (granulated) sugar
3 oz. ($\frac{3}{4}$ cup) plain (all-purpose) flour, sifted 3 times

Pre-heat oven to moderately hot (375°F, Gas Mark 5). Grease and paper-line two 7 in. sandwich tins (layer cake pans).
Melt the butter over a low heat and set aside.
Whisk the eggs and sugar over a basin or pan of hot water until thick, creamy and 3 times their original volume.
Pour the melted butter round the edge of the egg mixture (trying, if possible, to avoid pouring any sediment as well). Using a large metal spoon, fold in very gently until almost all of it is incorporated. Add half the flour and gently and lightly cut and fold into the mixture. Repeat with remaining flour.
Transfer to the prepared tins (pans) and bake near the top of the oven for 20–25 minutes or until well risen, golden and firm. Turn out onto a towel-covered wire (cake) rack.
Peel away the paper when completely cold and sandwich together with chosen filling.

Sandwich with oil

Make as traditional Genoese Sandwich (above) but omit the butter and fold in 3 tablespoons ($3\frac{3}{4}$ T) corn oil alternately with the sifted flour.

Genoese Cake

Make as traditional Genoese or Genoese with oil and transfer to a greased and paper-lined 7 in. round cake tin (pan).
Bake in the centre of a moderate oven (350°F, Gas Mark 4) for 45 minutes until well risen and firm. Turn out on to a teatowel-covered wire rack and carefully peel away the paper.
When completely cold, cut into 3 horizontal layers, fill with jam (preserves) and dust the top with castor (granulated) sugar.

Genoese Gateau

Make a Genoese Cake (above).
When cold, slice horizontally into 3 layers. Fill and decorate as suggested for other cakes in this section.

Genoese Iced Squares

Make as Traditional Genoese or Genoese with oil and transfer to a greased and paper-lined 6 in. square cake tin (pan).
Bake in the centre of moderate oven (350°F, Gas Mark 4) for 45–50 minutes until well risen and firm, or until a cocktail stick etc. inserted into the centre comes out clean.
Turn out on to a towel-covered wire (cake) rack and cut into squares when cold. Coat the tops with white glacé icing, made by mixing 6 oz. (1 cup) sifted icing (confectioners') sugar to a stiffish icing with water or strained fresh lemon juice. Allow the icing to trickle down the sides, then top each square with half a glacé cherry.

Lemon Chiffon Cake

4 oz. (1 cup) self-raising flour
5 oz. (10 T) castor (granulated) sugar
$\frac{1}{2}$ level teaspoon salt
4 tablespoons (5 T) corn oil
3 egg yolks
5 tablespoons ($6\frac{1}{4}$ T) water
$\frac{1}{2}$ teaspoon vanilla essence (extract)
Finely grated peel of $\frac{1}{2}$ a medium lemon
$\frac{1}{2}$ level teaspoon cream of tartar
3 egg whites

Pre-heat oven to warm (325°F, Gas Mark 3). Have ready a 7–8 in. ungreased deep ring tin (tube pan) with sloping sides.
Sift together the flour, sugar and salt. Make a well in the centre and add the oil, egg yolks, water, vanilla essence (extract) and lemon peel. Stir briskly until batter is smooth.
Add the cream of tartar to the egg whites and beat until stiff. (They should stand in peaks, but must not begin to break down or they will be difficult to fold into the batter.)
Pour the batter on to the egg whites and, using a metal spoon, fold in very gently, taking care not to stir the mixture. Pour into the prepared tin (pan) and bake in the centre of the oven for $1\frac{1}{4}$ hours. Invert the tin over a large funnel or bottle, and leave to stand until thoroughly cool, about 1 hour. To remove the cake, loosen the edges with a knife and tap the base of the tin (pan) sharply.

Vanilla Chiffon Cake

Make exactly as Lemon Chiffon Cake, but omit the lemon peel completely and increase the vanilla essence (extract) to 1 teaspoon.

Lemon chiffon cake (left)
Fruity soda loaf (above)

Fruity Soda Loaf

12 oz. (3 cups) plain (all-purpose) flour
1 level teaspoon salt
6 oz. ($\frac{3}{4}$ cup) castor (granulated) sugar
2 oz. ($\frac{1}{2}$ cup) walnuts, chopped
8 oz. ($1\frac{1}{2}$ cups) stoned (pitted) dates,
** chopped**
2 tablespoons ($2\frac{1}{2}$ T) corn oil
1 standard egg
1 level teaspoon bicarbonate of soda
** (baking soda)**
$\frac{1}{2}$ pint ($1\frac{1}{4}$ cups) boiling water

Pre-heat oven to moderate (350°F, Gas Mark 4). Well grease and paper-line a 2 lb. loaf tin (4 cup capacity oblong loaf pan). Brush the paper with more fat.

Sift together the flour and salt. Add the sugar, nuts and dates. Toss the ingredients lightly together to mix.

Whisk together the oil and egg. Dissolve the soda in the water and add to the dry ingredients with the whisked oil and egg. Stir briskly to form a smooth, slack mixture and transfer to the prepared tin (pan). Bake in the centre of the oven for $1\frac{1}{4}$–$1\frac{1}{2}$ hours or until well risen and firm. Leave in the tin (pan) for 5 minutes then turn out on to a wire cooling (cake) rack. Peel away the paper and leave the cake until completely cold.

To serve, cut into slices and spread with butter.

Spiced Fruity Soda Loaf

Make exactly as previous recipe, but sift the flour with 1 level teaspoon cinnamon, $\frac{1}{2}$ level teaspoon ground ginger and $\frac{1}{2}$ level teaspoon mixed spice.

Soda Loaf with Figs and Walnuts

Make exactly as Fruity Soda Loaf (above), but use the same amount of dried figs instead of the dates and 2 oz. ($\frac{1}{2}$ cup) coarsely chopped cashew or unsalted peanuts instead of the walnuts.

Gingerbreads and spicy cakes

Into this category fall an assortment of cakes which are made by the melting method, a technique whereby fat, syrup or treacle (molasses), sugar and sometimes water are melted together and combined with the dry ingredients to form, quickly and easily, a batter ready for baking.

Rubbing in, creaming and whisking are completely eliminated and these moist, flavourful cakes – with their spicy aroma – are traditional and much loved family favourites – especially in winter, round about Guy Fawkes time, Christmas and New Year.

In addition to these, some even simpler cakes do not require the liquids to be melted at all . . . but we will come to those later in the section.

Common Faults

Cake sunk in centre
1. Too much raising agent used.
2. Too much syrup or treacle (molasses) added.
3. Oven too hot or cake placed too high in oven.

Top shiny and texture close
1. Mixture beaten too much, too hard and too long.

Top cracked and texture dry
1. Not enough liquid added.
2. Too much raising agent used.
3. Oven too hot or shelf position too high.

Plain Gingerbread

4 oz. ($\frac{1}{2}$ cup) butter or margarine
2 oz. ($\frac{1}{4}$ cup) soft brown sugar
6 oz. ($\frac{1}{2}$ cup) black treacle (dark molasses)
2 oz. ($\frac{1}{4}$ cup) golden syrup (light corn syrup)
$\frac{1}{4}$ pint ($\frac{5}{8}$ cup) milk
2 standard eggs
8 oz. (2 cups) plain (all-purpose) flour
1 level teaspoon mixed spice
2 level teaspoons ground ginger
1 level teaspoon bicarbonate of soda (baking soda)

Pre-heat oven to cool (300°F, Gas Mark 2). Brush an 8 in. square tin (pan) with melted fat. Line the base and sides with greaseproof (waxed) paper and brush paper with more fat.

Put the butter or margarine, sugar, treacle (molasses) and syrup into a saucepan. Stir over a low heat until the fat has melted. Remove from heat, add the milk and cool. Beat the eggs and blend into the melted mixture. Sift the dry ingredients into a bowl. Add the liquid and stir briskly to combine the ingredients – *do not beat*. Pour into the prepared tin (pan). Bake in the centre of the oven for $1\frac{1}{4}$–$1\frac{1}{2}$ hours or until a cocktail stick etc. inserted into the centre comes out clean.

Store in an air-tight container when completely cold and leave for at least one day before cutting.

Prune Gingerbread

Make exactly as Plain Gingerbread but add 4 oz. (1 cup) pitted and chopped prunes with the cooled ingredients.

Fig and Nut Gingerbread

Make exactly as Plain Gingerbread but add 3 oz. ($\frac{3}{4}$ cup) chopped figs and 1 oz. ($\frac{1}{4}$ cup) chopped walnuts with the cooled ingredients.

Date and Orange Gingerbread

Make exactly as Plain Gingerbread but add 4 oz. (1 cup) chopped dates and 1 level teaspoon finely grated orange peel with the cooled ingredients.

Plain gingerbread

Wholemeal (Wholewheat) Gingerbread

Make exactly as Plain Gingerbread, but use 4 oz. (1 cup) plain (all-purpose) wholemeal (wholewheat) flour with 4 oz. (1 cup) plain (all-purpose) white flour.

Fruity Gingerbread

Make exactly as Plain Gingerbread, but add 4 oz. (1 cup) mixed dried fruits (currants, sultanas and raisins) and add with cooled ingredients.

Iced Nut Gingerbread

Make exactly as Plain Gingerbread but add 3 oz. ($\frac{3}{4}$ cup) blanched and chopped almonds with the cooled ingredients.

When completely cold, decorate with Lemon Glacé Icing: mix 6 oz. (1 cup) sifted icing (confectioners') sugar to a stiff icing with strained lemon juice. Spread over the top of the cold cake. When half set, decorate the edges with blanched and lightly toasted almonds. Stand 3 slices preserved ginger in the centre, (see page 62).

Crunchy Treacle Squares

3 oz. (6 T) butter
3 oz. (6 T) granulated sugar
3 oz. ($\frac{1}{4}$ cup) black treacle (dark molasses)
3 oz. ($\frac{1}{4}$ cup) golden syrup (light corn syrup)
6 oz. ($2\frac{1}{2}$–3 cups) porridge (rolled) oats

Pre-heat oven to warm (325°F, Gas Mark 3). Well grease a 7 × 11 in. Swiss roll tin (jelly roll pan).

Melt the butter slowly with the sugar, treacle (molasses) and syrup, but do not allow to boil. Remove from heat and stir in the oats.

Press into the prepared tin (pan) and bake in the centre of the oven for about 30 minutes.

Cut into squares when lukewarm then lift out of the tin (pan) on to a wire (cake) rack.

Store in an air-tight container when cold.

Chocolate Crackle Cake

8 oz. biscuits (graham crackers)
2 oz. ($\frac{1}{4}$ cup) butter
1 oz. (2 T) granulated sugar
1 tablespoon ($1\frac{1}{4}$ T) golden syrup (light corn syrup)
1 teaspoon vanilla essence (extract)
3 level dessertspoons (3 T) cocoa powder, sifted

Brush a loose-based (spring-form) 6 in. round cake tin (pan) with melted butter.

Line with greaseproof (waxed) paper and brush with more melted butter.

Break the biscuits into small pieces.

Put the butter, sugar and syrup into saucepan and melt over a low heat, without boiling.

Remove from heat, stir in the vanilla essence, cocoa and biscuits and transfer to the prepared tin (pan). Spread smoothly with a knife, cover with foil and refrigerate overnight.

Next day, turn out of the tin (pan) and cut into small portions.

Iced nut gingerbread
1 : Ingredients melting in saucepan

2 : Melted ingredients being stirred into dry ingredients

3 : Gingerbread mixture being poured into cake tin (pan)

4 : Baked gingerbread being tested with metal skewer

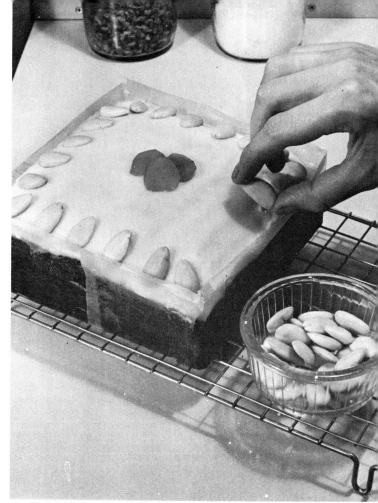

5 : Icing being spread over cake

6 : Top of gingerbread being decorated with nuts

7 : Completed cake

Barm Brack

$\frac{3}{4}$ pint (just under 2 cups) cold, strained tea
7 oz. ($\frac{7}{8}$ cup) soft brown sugar
12 oz. ($2\frac{1}{2}$ cups) mixed (chopped) dried fruit
10 oz. ($2\frac{1}{2}$ cups) self-raising flour
1 standard egg, beaten

Put the tea, sugar and dried fruit into a bowl. Cover and leave to soak overnight.
Sift the flour into a bowl and gradually blend in the egg and the tea mixture. Stir briskly, without beating, until smooth. Transfer to a greased and paper-lined 2 lb. loaf tin (4 cup capacity oblong loaf pan).
Bake in the centre of a moderate oven (350°F, Gas Mark 4) for about $1\frac{3}{4}$ hours. Turn out, when lukewarm, on to a wire (cake) rack.
When cold, cut into slices and spread with butter. Store any leftover cake in an air-tight container.

Ginger Tea Loaf

10 oz. ($2\frac{1}{2}$ cups) self-raising flour
2 level teaspoons ground ginger
$\frac{1}{2}$ level teaspoon mixed spice
4 oz. ($\frac{1}{2}$ cup) soft brown sugar
2 oz. ($\frac{1}{4}$ cup) lard or cooking fat (shortening)
3 oz. ($\frac{1}{4}$ cup) golden syrup (corn syrup)
3 oz. ($\frac{1}{4}$ cup) black treacle (dark molasses)
1 large egg, beaten
6 tablespoons ($7\frac{1}{2}$ T) milk

Pre-heat oven to warm (325°F, Gas Mark 3). Well grease a 2 lb. loaf tin (4 cup capacity oblong loaf pan). Line with greaseproof (waxed) paper then brush the paper with melted fat.
Sift the flour, ginger and spice into a bowl. Add the sugar and toss lightly together.
Melt the lard or cooking fat (shortening), syrup and treacle (molasses) over a low heat. Add to the dry ingredients with the egg and milk, stirring briskly not beating. When evenly combined, transfer to the prepared tin (pan).
Bake in the centre of the oven for $1\frac{1}{4}$–$1\frac{1}{2}$ hours until well risen and firm, or until a cocktail stick etc. inserted into the centre comes out clean. Leave in the tin (pan) for 5 minutes then cool on a wire (cake) rack. Store as above.

Ginger Tea Bread with Fruit

Make exactly as Ginger Tea Loaf (above) but add 5 oz. (1 cup) sultanas (golden raisins) to the dry ingredients.

Bournvita Loaf

$\frac{1}{2}$ pint ($1\frac{1}{4}$ cups) cold milk (or use skimmed milk granules (dry milk solids) and water)
10 oz. (2 cups) mixture of chopped dates, figs, sultanas (golden raisins) and currants
1 level teaspoon bicarbonate of soda (baking soda)
1 oz. (2 T) butter or margarine, melted
4 oz. ($\frac{1}{2}$ cup) castor (granulated) sugar
2 oz. Bournvita (malted chocolate powder)
1 standard egg, beaten
10 oz. ($2\frac{1}{2}$ cups) self-raising flour, sifted

Pre-heat oven to moderate (350°F, Gas Mark 4). Brush a 2 lb. loaf tin (4 cup capacity oblong loaf pan) with melted fat. Line the base and sides with greaseproof (waxed) paper and brush the paper with more fat. Bring the milk slowly to the boil, stirring. Put the fruit, soda, butter or margarine, sugar and Bournvita into a bowl. Pour on the boiling milk and mix well. Add the beaten egg then gradually fold in the sifted flour. When the mixture is smooth and evenly combined, transfer to the prepared tin (pan).
Bake in the centre of the oven for about 1 hour until well risen and golden, or until a cocktail stick etc. inserted into the centre comes out clean. Leave in the tin (pan) for 5 minutes then turn out on to a wire (cake) rack.
Store in an air-tight container when cold.

Orange and Almond Tea Bread

12 oz. (3 cups) self-raising flour
$\frac{1}{2}$ level teaspoon salt
1 level teaspoon cinnamon
2 oz. ($\frac{1}{4}$ cup) blanched almonds, chopped
Finely grated peel of 1 small orange
3 oz. (6 T) castor (granulated) sugar
2 medium eggs, beaten
$\frac{1}{2}$ pint ($1\frac{1}{4}$ cups) cold milk *less* 1 tablespoon ($1\frac{1}{4}$ T)
2 oz. ($\frac{1}{4}$ cup) butter, melted

Pre-heat oven to moderate (350°F, Gas Mark 4). Brush a 2 lb. loaf tin (4 cup capacity oblong loaf pan) with melted fat. Line the base and sides with greaseproof (waxed) paper then brush the paper with more fat. Sift the flour, salt and cinnamon into a bowl. Add the almonds, orange peel and sugar. Mix to a soft batter with the beaten egg and milk, then gently stir in the melted butter.

Transfer to the prepared tin (pan) and bake in the centre of the oven for 1 hour until well risen and golden, or until a cocktail stick etc. inserted into the centre comes out clean. Leave in the tin (pan) for 5 minutes then turn out and cool on a wire (cake) rack.

Peel away the paper and store in an air-tight container when cold.

Lemon and Sultana Coffee Bread

Make exactly as Orange and Almond Tea Bread (above), substituting 2 oz. ($\frac{1}{2}$ cup) sultanas (golden raisins) for the nuts and adding 1–2 level teaspoons finely grated lemon peel instead of the orange peel.

Apricot Coffee Bread

12 oz. (3 cups) self-raising flour
$\frac{1}{2}$ level teaspoon salt
3 oz. (6 T) castor (granulated) sugar
5 oz. (1 cup) dried apricots, soaked overnight and chopped
2 oz. ($\frac{1}{2}$ cup) blanched almonds, chopped
Finely grated peel of 1 small orange
2 standard eggs, beaten
8–9 tablespoons (10–11 T) milk
2 oz. ($\frac{1}{4}$ cup) butter, melted

Pre-heat oven to warm (325°F, Gas Mark 3). Brush a 2 lb. loaf tin (4 cup capacity oblong loaf pan) with melted fat. Line the base and sides with greaseproof (waxed) paper then brush the paper with more fat. Sift the flour and salt into bowl. Add the sugar, apricots, almonds and orange peel. Make a well in the centre. Combine the remaining ingredients and pour into the well. Mix to a soft dropping consistency, stirring briskly without beating.

Transfer to the prepared tin (pan) and bake in the centre of the oven for $1\frac{1}{2}$ hours until well risen and firm, or until cocktail stick etc. inserted into the centre comes out clean. Leave in the tin (pan) for 5 minutes then turn out and cool on a wire (cake) rack.

Peel away the paper and store in an air-tight container when cold.

Prune and Walnut Coffee Bread

Make exactly as above, using 5 oz. (1 cup) pitted and chopped prunes and 2 oz. ($\frac{1}{2}$ cup) chopped walnuts.

Party pineapple and walnut coffee bread

Party Pineapple and Walnut Coffee Bread

12 oz. (3 cups) self-raising flour
$\frac{1}{2}$ level teaspoon salt
3 oz. (6 T) castor (granulated) sugar
8 oz. canned pineapple slices, well-drained
2 oz. ($\frac{1}{2}$ cup) walnuts
2 standard eggs, beaten
8–9 tablespoons (10–11 T) milk
2 oz. ($\frac{1}{4}$ cup) butter, melted
Icing
6 oz. (1 cup) icing (confectioners') sugar, sifted
Warm water

Pre-heat oven to warm (325°F, Gas Mark 3). Brush a 2 lb. loaf tin (4 cup capacity oblong loaf pan) with melted fat. Line the base and sides with greaseproof (waxed) paper and brush with more fat. Sift together the flour and salt then add the sugar.

Reserve 2 pineapple slices and 4 walnut halves for decoration. Chop the remainder coarsely and add to the dry ingredients. Make a well in the centre.

Blend together the eggs, milk and butter then stir into the dry ingredients to make a soft dropping consistency.

Transfer to the prepared tin (pan) and bake in the centre of the oven for $1\frac{1}{2}$ hours until well-risen and golden, or until a cocktail stick etc. inserted into the centre comes out clean.

Leave in the tin (pan) for 5 minutes then turn out and cool on a wire (cake) rack. Leave until completely cold.

To make icing: mix the sifted sugar to a thickish icing with water, stirring briskly without beating. Pour over the cake, allowing it to trickle down the sides and find its own level.

When half-set, cut the reserved pineapple slices in half and arrange on top of the cake with a walnut half between each.

Golden cake (left) Ginger tea loaf (above) Cider crumble cake (below)

Cider Crumble Cake

1 lb. 2 oz. (4½ cups) self-raising flour
Dash of salt
4 oz. (½ cup) soft brown sugar
2½ oz. (½ cup) chopped dates
3 tablespoons (3¾ T) black treacle (dark molasses)
½ pint (1¼ cups) cider (apple cider)
2 standard eggs, beaten

Topping
1½ oz. (3 T) butter
1½ oz. (6 T) plain (all-purpose) flour
1½ oz. (3 T) castor (granulated) sugar
1½ oz. (3 T) chopped walnuts
½ level teaspoon cinnamon
3 tablespoons (3¾ T) plum jam (preserves)

Pre-heat oven to warm (325°F, Gas Mark 3). Well grease a 9 in. square tin (pan). Line the base and sides with greased greaseproof (waxed) paper.
Sift the flour and salt into a bowl. Add the sugar and dates. Heat the treacle (molasses) and cider gently until the treacle (molasses) has dissolved. Stir the cider mixture and eggs into the flour. Mix well. Transfer to the prepared tin (pan) and bake in the centre of the oven for 30 minutes.
For topping: rub together the butter, flour and sugar. Mix in walnuts and cinnamon.
Remove the cake from the oven, spread with jam (preserves) and sprinkle with the nut crumble.
Return to the oven for a further 20 minutes, or until a cocktail stick etc. inserted into the centre comes out clean.
Leave in the tin (pan) for 10 minutes, then turn out on to a wire rack. When completely cold, wrap in foil and leave 2 days before cutting.

Fudge Frosted Spice Cake

10 oz. (2½ cups) plain (all-purpose) flour
½ level teaspoon salt
1½ level teaspoons ground ginger
¾ level teaspoon bicarbonate of soda (baking soda)
3 oz. (¾ cup) lard or cooking fat (shortening)
3 oz. (6 T) soft brown sugar
3 tablespoons (3¾ T) golden syrup (light corn syrup)
1 standard egg
¼ pint (⅝ cup) milk
4 oz. (just under 1 cup) mixed (chopped) dried fruit
1 oz. (3 pieces) preserved ginger, sliced

Fudge Icing
3 oz. (6 T) butter
3 tablespoons (3¾ T) milk
1 tablespoon liquid coffee essence (strong coffee)
Dash of salt
1 lb (2½ cups) icing (confectioners') sugar, sifted
Approximately 25 chocolate buttons for decoration

Pre-heat oven to moderate (350°F, Gas Mark 4). Brush a 7 in. round cake tin (pan) with melted fat. Line the base and sides with greaseproof (waxed) paper and brush with more fat.
Sift the flour, salt, ginger and soda into a bowl. Put the fat and sugar into pan with the syrup. Leave over a moderate heat until melted. Beat the egg and milk together.

Add the fruit and ginger to the dry ingredients. Pour in the melted sugar mixture then add the egg and milk. Stir briskly without beating to form a smooth batter.

Transfer to the prepared tin (pan), make a shallow well in the centre and bake in the centre of the oven for $1\frac{3}{4}$–2 hours or until well-risen and firm, or until a cocktail stick etc. inserted into the centre comes out clean.

Leave in the tin (pan) for about 10 minutes then turn out on to a wire cooling (cake) rack. Peel away the paper.

To make icing: put the butter, milk, essence (coffee) and salt into a saucepan and stir over a low heat until the butter is melted; do not allow to boil. Pour over the sifted sugar. Mix thoroughly, leave until almost cold then beat until thick enough to coat the back of a spoon.

Level the top of the cake (if necessary), turn over on the wire (cake) rack and coat the top and sides with frosting. Decorate with chocolate buttons.

Golden Cake

1 small packet instant mashed potato
$1\frac{1}{2}$ level teaspoons baking powder
3 oz. (6 T) margarine
1 level tablespoon ($1\frac{1}{4}$ T) golden syrup (light corn syrup)
3 oz. (6 T) castor (granulated) sugar
Finely grated peel and juice of 1 medium orange
2 standard eggs, separated
Piece of candied peel for decoration

Pre-heat oven to moderate (350°F, Gas Mark 4). Brush a 6 in. round cake tin (pan) with melted white cooking fat (shortening). Line the base and sides with greaseproof (waxed) paper and brush with more fat. Place the powdered potato and baking powder into a bowl.

Melt the margarine, syrup, sugar and grated peel and juice of the orange in a saucepan. Heat gently until the sugar has dissolved, stirring occasionally. Remove from heat and pour on to the potato mixture. Beat well. Stir in the egg yolks. Whisk the egg whites to a stiff snow and gently fold into the potato mixture with a large metal spoon. Transfer to the prepared tin (pan) and bake in the centre of the oven for about 45 minutes until well risen, golden and firm to the touch. Halfway through cooking time, place the peel on top of the cake and cover with paper to avoid over-browning. Leave the cake in the tin (pan) for 5 minutes before turning out on to a wire (cake) rack.

Store in an air-tight container when cold.

Parkin

8 oz. (2 cups) plain (all-purpose) flour
$\frac{1}{2}$ level teaspoon salt
1 level teaspoon each cinnamon and mixed spice
$\frac{1}{2}$ level teaspoon ground ginger
8 oz. (just under $1\frac{1}{2}$ cups) medium oatmeal
5 oz. (10 T) cooking fat (shortening) or butter
4 oz. ($\frac{1}{2}$ cup) soft brown sugar
4 oz. ($\frac{1}{3}$ cup) golden syrup (light corn syrup)
4 oz. ($\frac{1}{3}$ cup) black treacle (dark molasses)
1 standard egg, beaten
$\frac{1}{4}$ pint ($\frac{5}{8}$ cup) milk

Pre-heat oven to warm (325°F, Gas Mark 3). Brush a 9 in. square cake tin (pan) or shallow roasting pan with melted fat. Line the base and sides with greaseproof (waxed) paper and brush with more fat. Sift the flour, salt and spices into a bowl. Add the oatmeal and toss lightly together.

Put the fat, sugar, syrup and treacle (molasses) in a saucepan and leave over a low heat until the fat melts. Add to the dry ingredients with the beaten egg and milk and mix to a soft consistency, stirring briskly without beating.

Transfer to the prepared tin (pan) and bake in the centre of the oven for $1\frac{1}{2}$–$1\frac{3}{4}$ hours or until a cocktail stick etc. inserted into the centre comes out clean. Leave in the tin (pan) for 10 minutes, then turn out and cool on a wire (cake) rack.

Store in an air-tight container when completely cold and leave for at least one day before cutting into squares and serving.

Ginger Nuts

3 oz. (6 T) butter
3 oz. (6 T) soft brown sugar
3 oz. ($\frac{1}{4}$ cup) golden syrup (light corn syrup)
8 oz. (2 cups) plain (all-purpose) flour
2 level teaspoons ground ginger
$\frac{1}{2}$ level teaspoon each cinnamon and mixed spice
$\frac{1}{4}$ level teaspoon salt
1 level teaspoon bicarbonate of soda (baking soda)
1 tablespoon ($1\frac{1}{4}$ T) warm water

Pre-heat oven to warm (325°F, Gas Mark 3). Brush two large baking trays (sheets) with melted fat.

Put the butter, sugar and syrup into a pan and melt over a low heat. Sift the flour, spices and salt into a bowl. Make a well in the centre. Add

Fudge frosted spice cake

Apple strudel

the melted ingredients and the soda dissolved in the warm water. Mix thoroughly with fork then form into 24 equal-sized balls. Put on to the prepared baking trays (sheets), leaving room between each for spreading.

Bake just below and just above the centre of the oven for 8 minutes. Reverse the trays (sheets) and bake for a further 8–10 minutes. Leave to stand for a few minutes before transferring to a wire (cake) rack.

Store in an air-tight container when cold.

Brandy Snaps

2 oz. ($\frac{1}{4}$ cup) butter
2 oz. (4 T) granulated sugar
2$\frac{1}{2}$ oz. ($\frac{1}{4}$ cup) golden (light corn) syrup
2 oz. ($\frac{1}{2}$ cup) plain (all-purpose) flour
1 level teaspoon ground ginger
$\frac{1}{2}$ level teaspoon mixed spice
2 teaspoons lemon juice
About $\frac{1}{4}$ pint ($\frac{5}{8}$ cup) double cream (whipping cream)

Pre-heat oven to warm (325°F, Gas Mark 3). Well grease two large baking trays (sheets).

Put the butter, sugar and syrup in a saucepan and melt over a low heat. Sift the flour and spices together. Add to the melted ingredients with the lemon juice. Stir briskly, without beating, until the batter is evenly combined.

Drop 8 teaspoons of the mixture (well apart as they spread out) on to one of the prepared trays (sheets). Bake in the centre of the oven for 8 minutes.

Leave about 30 seconds then lift each off with a spatula or large, round-topped knife and roll fairly quickly round the greased handle of a wooden spoon. Slide off handle and transfer to a wire (cake) rack.

Repeat, using up the remaining mixture (about 16 brandy snaps in all). When completely cold, fill both ends of each with whipped cream.

Note : Should brandy snaps harden up on the tray before you have a chance to roll them, return to the oven for 1–2 minutes.

top left : Cream cheese and strawberry flan
(front) and hazelnut layer cake (behind)
Fudge cake (top right)
French chocolate squares (below)

Continental cakes

Happy memories from holidays abroad may include – besides sunshine, novel and exotic foods and breath-taking panoramas – a bewildering array of luscious, rich cakes and pastries in which Continentals revel!

Throughout Europe, cafés are packed tight, summer and winter, with locals – and tourists if they can cope – devouring, with marked concentration and almost holy devotion, gargantuan portions of creamy sweetness and obviously relishing every single minute of it!

Because of limitations of space I give here just a short selection of a few specialities from abroad. I hope you will be tempted to try one or two.

Apple Strudel – Austria

8 oz. (2 cups) plain (all-purpose) flour
Dash of salt
4 dessertspoons (4 T) salad oil
¼ pint (⅝ cup) lukewarm water

Filling
3 oz. (6 T) butter, melted
4 level dessertspoons (4 T) *each* **fresh white breadcrumbs and ground almonds**
2 lb. (about 3 large) cooking apples, peeled, cored and very thinly sliced
2 level teaspoons cinnamon
4 level tablespoons (5 T) castor (granulated) sugar
2 tablespoons (2½ T) dark rum (optional)
2 heaped tablespoons (2½ T) flaked or blanched and chopped almonds
4 oz. (just under 1 cup) sultanas (golden raisins)
Icing (confectioners') sugar to dust

Sift the flour and salt into a bowl. Make a well in the centre then add the oil and water. Mix to soft dough with fingertips. Turn out on to a floured surface and knead *thoroughly* until the dough is no longer sticky, but smooth and elastic, about 30 minutes – regretfully there are no shortcuts! Return the dough to bowl, cover and leave to 'relax' at kitchen temperature for 30 minutes.

Put a clean, patterned tablecloth or large pat-terned tea-towel on a kitchen table or work surface. Dredge heavily with flour. Stand the dough in centre of the cloth, then roll out – in all directions – as thinly as possible, starting from the middle of the dough and working outwards.

As soon as the pattern of the cloth starts showing through, stop rolling and start pulling. Gently, with fingertips, pull until the edges are as paper thin as the centre part, taking care not to break the dough or get large holes in it. The ball of dough should now be a large sheet with a raggedy edge, ready for filling.

Brush all over with the melted butter then sprinkle with half the breadcrumbs and ground almonds. Put the apples into a bowl and toss with the cinnamon, sugar and rum if used. Spread over the dough, leaving a 1 in. margin uncovered round the edges. Trickle all but a couple of teaspoons butter over the apples, then sprinkle with the remaining breadcrumbs and ground almonds, flaked almonds and sultanas (golden raisins). Fold the uncovered edges over the filling for neatness, then carefully roll up the Strudel as for a Swiss roll (jelly roll). Roll it from the cloth on to buttered baking tray (sheet), brush with the remaining butter, then bake in the centre of a moderately hot oven (375°F, Gas Mark 5) for about 35–45 minutes. Leave on the tray (sheet) to cool. When lukewarm, dredge with sifted icing (confectioners') sugar and cut into diagonal slices. Serve while still slightly warm and accompany, if desired, with softly whipped cream or ice cream.

Shortcut Strudel

Some Continental shops and delicatessen counters of supermarkets sell packets of Strudel pastry which, if you want to save time, is a fair and reasonable substitute for the real thing.

Cheese and Cherry Strudel – Austria

Make exactly as Apple Strudel (above) but instead of using apple as a filling, beat 1 lb. curd (cottage) cheese with 2 egg yolks, 4 tablespoons (5 T) single cream (coffee cream), 3 level tablespoons ($3\frac{3}{4}$ T) castor (granulated) sugar, 1 teaspoon vanilla essence (extract) and a dash of salt.

Spread over the pastry to within 1 in. of edges, then stud generously with pitted cherries (homestewed or canned), making sure they are well-drained. Roll up, brush with melted butter and bake as Apple Strudel, allowing about 10 minutes less baking time.

Cherry Flan – Holland

6 oz. ($1\frac{1}{2}$ cups) plain (all-purpose) flour
Dash of salt
4 oz. ($\frac{1}{4}$ cup) Dutch (sweet) butter
2 oz. (4 T) castor (granulated) sugar
1 egg yolk
1 medium (1 pound) can Morello or dark red cherries
1 heaped teaspoon ($\frac{1}{2}$ T) arrowroot or cornflour (cornstarch)
$\frac{1}{4}$ pint ($\frac{5}{8}$ cup) cherry syrup from can
$\frac{1}{2}$ pint ($1\frac{1}{4}$ cups) double cream (whipping cream)

Pre-heat oven to moderately hot (400°F, Gas Mark 6). Well butter a 10 in. flan tin (springform pan), or stand a 10 in. flan ring on a lightly greased baking tray (sheet).

Sift the flour and salt into a bowl. Cut in the butter with a pastry cutter or round-topped knife, then rub into the dry ingredients with fingertips. Add the sugar, then mix to a stiff paste with the egg yolk and a few teaspoons water if pastry is on the dry and crumbly side. Press, without rolling, into the prepared flan tin (pan) or ring and prick the base with a fork.

Line the base and sides with foil to prevent pastry from rising as it cooks, then bake in the centre of the oven for 15 minutes. Remove the foil and bake for a further 15 minutes or until golden. Leave for 10 minutes before removing carefully from the tin (pan) or lifting off the flan ring.

When completely cold, fill the pastry case with cherries then make a glaze by blending the arrowroot or cornflour (cornstarch) with the cherry syrup and heating till it thickens, stirring continuously. Allow to cool slightly before spooning over the cherries. Decorate generously with freshly whipped cream.

Note : For a more lavish flan, use 2 cans drained cherries.

Hazelnut Layer Cake – Denmark

$2\frac{1}{2}$ oz. (5 T) Danish (sweet) butter
4 oz. ($\frac{1}{4}$ cup) castor (granulated) sugar
3 standard eggs
4 oz. (1 cup) self-raising flour, sifted 3 times

Filling
4 oz. ($\frac{1}{4}$ cup) Danish (sweet) butter
8 oz. ($1\frac{1}{2}$ cups) icing (confectioners') sugar, sifted
1 dessertspoon (1 T) milk or liquid coffee essence (strong coffee) if preferred
2 oz. ($\frac{1}{2}$ cup) finely chopped hazelnuts
8 whole hazelnuts for decoration

Pre-heat oven to moderately hot (400°F, Gas Mark 6).

Melt the butter and leave on one side.

Whisk the sugar and eggs over a bowl of hot water until they treble in volume, become much paler in colour and as thick as softly whipped cream. Pour the butter round the edge of the egg mixture and, using a metal spoon, gently fold in alternately with half the flour. Gently fold in the remaining flour, then divide mixture equally between two 8 in. sandwich tins (pans). Bake just above the centre of the oven for 10–12 minutes or until well risen and golden and just beginning to shrink away from the sides of the tins (pans). Turn out on to a towel-covered wire (cake) rack and gently peel away paper. Leave until cold then cut each in half horizontally.

Make butter cream: beat the butter until soft then gradually beat in the sifted sugar. Continue beating until light and fluffy, then add the milk or coffee essence (strong coffee).

Sandwich the cake together with some of the butter cream, spread more cream over the top and sides. Press the hazelnuts against the sides then, using an icing (pastry) bag and star-shaped tube, pipe 8 rosettes or remaining butter cream on top of the cake. Top each rosette with a hazelnut.

Overleaf : Mocha cream meringue layer

Chocolate drop fudge cake

Chocolate Drop Fudge Cake – Belgium

Make exactly as Fudge Cake (below), but press the mixture into a 6 in. round cake tin (pan), base-lined with foil.

After turning out of the tin (pan), cover with butter cream, made by creaming 4 oz. ($\frac{1}{2}$ cup) butter with 6 oz. (1 cup) sifted icing (confectioners') sugar. Press chocolate vermicelli against the sides and decorate the top with piped rosettes of butter cream and chocolate drops.

Cream Cheese and Strawberry Flan – Denmark

5 oz. (1$\frac{1}{4}$ cups) plain (all-purpose) flour
Dash of salt
3 oz. (6 T) Danish (sweet) butter
2 oz. (4 T) castor (granulated) sugar
1 egg yolk

Filling
3–4 oz. cream cheese
2 tablespoons (2$\frac{1}{2}$ T) single cream (coffee cream)
12 oz. (2 cups) strawberries
3 level tablespoons (3$\frac{3}{4}$ T) redcurrant jelly

Pre-heat oven to moderately hot (400°F, Gas Mark 6).
Sift the flour and salt into a bowl. Add the butter and cut into the dry ingredients with a pastry cutter or round-topped knife. Rub in lightly with fingertips. Add the sugar and egg yolk then draw mixture together to form a paste. Press into an 8 in. fluted flan ring standing on an ungreased baking tray (cookie sheet), then line

with foil to prevent pastry rising as it cooks. Bake in the centre of the oven for 15 minutes. Remove the foil then return the flan case to the upper part of the oven for a further 7–10 minutes or until golden. Remove from the oven, leave for 5 minutes, then lift off the flan ring. Leave the pastry until cold before filling.
Beat the cheese and cream together until smooth. Spread over the base of the flan then fill with whole strawberries.
A little while before serving, melt the redcurrant jelly and brush over the fruit.

Fudge Cake – Belgium

4 oz. ($\frac{1}{2}$ cup) butter
2 tablespoons (2$\frac{1}{2}$ T) golden syrup (light corn syrup)
8 oz. (2 cups) crushed sweet biscuits (lady fingers)
1 oz. (3 T) seedless raisins
2 tablespoons (2$\frac{1}{2}$ T) glacé cherries, quartered
5 oz. (5 squares) plain (semi-sweet) chocolate, chopped

Fudge Icing
2 oz. (2 squares) plain (bitter) chocolate
1 oz. (2 T) butter
3 dessertspoons (3 T) water
6 oz. (1 cup) icing (confectioners') sugar
Extra icing (confectioners') sugar and chocolate to decorate (optional)

Grease and line the base of 1 lb. loaf tin (2 cup capacity oblong loaf pan) with a piece of buttered foil.
Melt the butter and syrup in a saucepan. Stir in the biscuits, fruit and chocolate. Press firmly into the prepared tin (pan) and leave in a cool place until set. Turn out on to a board.
For Fudge Icing: melt the chocolate and butter with the water over a basin of hot water. Remove from heat, stir in the sifted sugar and beat until cool and thick.

Layered hazelnut cream meringue

Spread over the cake. Dust with sifted icing (confectioners') sugar and decorate with extra melted chocolate if desired.

French Chocolate Squares

8 oz. (8 squares) plain (semi sweet) chocolate
1 lb. sweet plain biscuits (sugar cookies), crushed
3 oz. (6 T) castor (granulated) sugar
4 oz. (1 cup) chopped walnuts
2 oz. ($\frac{1}{4}$ cup) butter
1 tablespoon ($1\frac{1}{4}$ T) rum, brandy or liquid coffee essence (strong coffee)
1 small can less 1 tablespoon ($6\frac{1}{2}$ oz. can) evaporated milk
2 standard eggs, beaten

Fudge Icing
See Belgian Fudge Cake (page 76).

Oil an 8 in. shallow square cake tin (pan). Line with foil, allowing it to extend about 1 in. above the top edge of the tin (pan). Brush with melted butter.

Break up the chocolate, put into a bowl standing over a pan of hot water and leave until melted.

Put the crushed biscuits into a bowl. Add the sugar and walnuts. Melt the butter then stir in the alcohol or essence (coffee) and milk. Gradually blend into the melted chocolate with the beaten eggs.

Pour on to the biscuit crumb mixture and stir thoroughly to combine. Transfer to the prepared tin (pan) and refrigerate overnight, until firm and set.

Before serving, ease the cake out of the tin (pan), peel away the foil and cover the top with Fudge Icing. When the icing has set, cut the cake into wedges.

Keep any left-over cake in the refrigerator.

Layered Hazelnut Cream Meringue – France

3 egg whites
Dash of lemon juice or cream of tartar
7 oz. (14 T) castor (granulated) sugar
1 level tablespoon ($1\frac{1}{4}$ T) cornflour (cornstarch)

Filling
$\frac{1}{2}$ pint ($1\frac{1}{4}$ cups) double cream (whipping cream)
2 oz. ($\frac{1}{2}$ cup) hazelnuts, coarsely chopped
2 tablespoons grated chocolate
About 1 dozen whole hazelnuts for decoration

Pre-heat oven to very cool (225°F, Gas Mark $\frac{1}{4}$). Brush 2 large baking trays (cookie sheets) with salad oil. Cover with a double thickness of greaseproof (waxed) paper *but do not brush the paper with oil.*

Put the egg whites and lemon juice or cream of tartar into a large, clean, dry bowl. Beat to a stiff snow. Gradually add half the sugar and continue beating until the meringue is shiny and stands in high firm peaks when the beaters are lifted out of the bowl. Gently fold in the remaining sugar alternately with the cornflour (cornstarch).

Spread the mixture into three 7 in. rounds on the prepared trays. Bake in the centre and lower part of the oven until firm, crisp and set, but still almost white, about 3 hours or perhaps a little longer. Change the trays round after $1\frac{1}{2}$ hours.

When nearly cold, lift carefully off paper and put back upside down. Return to oven (heat off) for about an hour to dry out completely.

Beat the cream until thick and fold in the nuts. Sandwich the meringue layers thickly with the cream then pile rest on top. Sprinkle with chocolate and decorate with hazelnuts.

Mocha Cream Meringue Layer – France

Make exactly as previous recipe, but pipe about 7 whirls of meringue on to one of the baking trays (sheets) in addition to the 3 rounds. When cold, sandwich the layers together with Mocha Butter Cream: beat 6 oz. ($\frac{3}{4}$ cup) butter until soft, then gradually beat in 12 oz. ($2\frac{1}{2}$ cups) sifted icing (confectioners') sugar alternately with 1 level tablespoon ($1\frac{1}{4}$ T) cocoa powder mixed to a thickish paste with hot strong coffee and allowed to cool.

Place the small meringues on top, holding them in position with Mocha Butter Cream.

Covered Apple Cake – Germany

Line an 8 in. spring form tin (pan) standing on ungreased baking tray (sheet) with home-made or commercial flaky or puff pastry.

Fill with thickly stewed apples, sweetened to taste with sugar and flavoured with a little rum.

Brush the pastry edges with water then cover with a lid, rolled and cut from pastry. Press edges well together to seal, then mark into wedges with back of knife. Brush with beaten egg and bake on shelf above centre in a hot oven (425°F, Gas Mark 7) for about 20–30 minutes or until well-puffed and golden.

Remove from the oven, unclip the sides of the tin (pan) and allow the cake to cool. Cut into wedges when cold.

Cheesecake – Central Europe and Jewish

About 6 tablespoons (7½ T) crushed digestive biscuits (graham crackers)
1½ lb. curd (cottage) cheese
Finely grated peel and juice of 1 medium lemon
1 teaspoon vanilla essence (extract)
6 oz. (¾ cup) castor (granulated) sugar
2 level tablespoons (2½ T) cornflour (cornstarch)
3 standard eggs, separated
¼ pint (⅝ cup) double cream (whipping cream)

Pre-heat oven to warm (325°F, Gas Mark 3). Brush an 8 in. spring form tin (pan) with butter and sprinkle heavily with crushed biscuits. Beat the cheese until smooth with the lemon peel and juice, sugar, vanilla essence (extract), cornflour (cornstarch) and egg yolks.

Beat the egg whites to a stiff snow. Beat the cream until thick. Using a large metal spoon, fold the whites and cream alternately into the cheese mixture. When smooth and evenly combined, transfer to the prepared tin (pan) and bake in the centre of the oven for 45 minutes.

Turn off the heat, open the oven door and leave the cake for a further 30 minutes. Remove from the oven, unclip the sides of the tin (pan) when the cake is completely cold.

For a browner top (as in photograph) cook near the top of the oven for about 35–40 minutes, but watch the cake carefully as it might brown too much in this position.

For serving, leave the cake on its metal spring form base.

Fruited Cheesecake

If liked, add 2 tablespoons (2½ T) sultanas (golden raisins) or seedless raisins to the cheese mixture before folding in the cream and egg whites.

Cheesecake (below)
Covered apple cake (right)

Chilled cheesecake

Sour Cream Topped Cheesecake

For an even richer effect, remove the cake from the oven when cooked and cover with $\frac{1}{4}$ pint ($\frac{5}{8}$ cup) soured cream. Return to the oven (with the heat off) for a further 30 minutes.

Decorated Cheesecake

Make Sour Cream Topped Cheesecake. Just before serving, sprinkle with powdered cinnamon, chopped and toasted almonds, chopped pistachio nuts, chopped pecan nuts or grated chocolate. One of my own favourites is the lightest dusting of very finely ground coffee, but I know this is not everybody's taste!

Chilled Cheesecake

4 oz. ($\frac{1}{2}$ cup) butter
1 packet (8 oz.) digestive biscuits (graham crackers)
4 level teaspoons (2 envelopes plain) gelatine (gelatin)
1 small (1-pound) can crushed pineapple (pineapple chunks)
1 lb. (about 2 cups) cottage cheese
$\frac{1}{4}$ pint ($\frac{5}{8}$ cup) double cream (whipping cream)
2 standard eggs, separated
4 oz. ($\frac{1}{2}$ cup) castor (granulated) sugar
Finely grated peel and juice of 1 lemon

Decoration
$\frac{1}{2}$ glacé cherry
Pineapple pieces
Angelica

Brush a loose-based 8 in. round cake tin (spring-form pan) with corn oil. Melt the butter and stir in the crushed biscuits. Press thickly over the base of the tin (pan).

Soften the gelatine (gelatin) in 4 tablespoons (5 T) of the pineapple syrup then dissolve over a very low heat.

Press the cheese through a fine mesh sieve into a large bowl. Beat the cream until thick then fold into the cheese with the egg yolks, sugar, lemon peel and juice and melted gelatine (gelatin). Mix thoroughly.

When cold and only *just* beginning to thicken, stir in the well drained pineapple pieces (reserving about 12 for decoration) and the egg whites, beaten to a stiff snow. Transfer to the prepared tin (pan) and refrigerate until firm and set.

To remove from the tin (pan), dip quickly into boiling water, stand on top of a flat-lidded heavy container and gently push the sides of the tin (pan) downwards.

Decorate the top with a flower and stem formed from the pineapple pieces, cherry and angelica.

Chilled Fruit Cocktail Cheesecake – Central Europe and United States

Make exactly as above, but use 1 small (1-pound) can of well drained fruit cocktail instead of the pineapple pieces. Decorate the top with a border of canned peach slices and make a flower pattern on top with pieces of peach slices, glacé cherries and angelica.

Redcurrant Cheesecake – Central Europe and United States

Make up the Chilled Cheesecake mixture (above), but use half quantities of ingredients and omit the pineapple altogether. Soften and dissolve the gelatine (gelatin) in 2 tablespoons ($2\frac{1}{2}$ T) water.

To make crunchy base: melt 3 oz. (6 T) butter with 3 tablespoons ($3\frac{3}{4}$ T) golden syrup (light corn syrup). Stir in 6 oz. (4 cups) crushed cornflakes then press over the base and sides of an 8 in. greased flan ring standing on lightly greased baking tray (sheet).

Bake in the centre of moderate oven (350°F, Gas Mark 4) for 10 minutes. Carefully lift off the flan ring when the cornflake case is cold and transfer to a serving plate.

Fill with the cheese mixture (which should be just on the point of setting) and chill until firm. Just before serving, tip with stewed redcurrants (well drained), then brush with 2 tablespoons ($2\frac{1}{2}$ T) melted redcurrant jelly. Pipe a border of whipped cream on the outside edge.

Note: If preferred, fruit pie filling may be used instead of redcurrants.

Redcurrant cheesecake

Yogurt and Orange Cake – Bulgaria

6 oz. (1½ cups) self-raising flour
Dash of salt
4 oz. (½ cup) butter
6 oz. (¾ cup) castor (granulated) sugar
2 standard eggs
½ drum (3 oz.) frozen orange juice
  concentrate, thawed
¼ pint (⅝ cup) natural (plain) yogurt

Orange Filling and Topping
2 oz. (¼ cup) butter
6 oz. (just over 1 cup) icing (confectioners')
  sugar, sifted
About 2 tablespoons (2½ T) frozen orange
  juice concentrate, thawed
Crystallized orange slices

Pre-heat oven to moderately hot (375°F, Gas Mark 5). Brush two 8 in. sandwich tins (layer cake pans) with melted butter, then line base and sides with greaseproof (waxed) paper. Brush with more butter.
Sift the flour and salt into a bowl.
Cream the butter and sugar together until light and fluffy then beat in the whole eggs, one at a time, adding a dessertspoon (tablespoon) sifted dry ingredients with each. Fold in the remaining flour alternately with orange juice concentrate and yogurt.
When thoroughly mixed, transfer to the prepared tins (pans) and bake in the centre of the oven for 30–35 minutes or until well-risen, golden and firm. Turn out and cool on a wire (cake) rack.

To make filling and topping: beat the butter until soft then gradually beat in the sugar alternately with the orange juice concentrate.
When the mixture is light and fluffy, use half to sandwich the cakes together and half to cover the top of cake. Decorate attractively with crystallized orange slices.

Sachertorte – Austria

10 oz. (10 squares) plain (semi-sweet)
  chocolate
1 tablespoon (1¼ T) liquid coffee essence
  (strong coffee)
1 teaspoon vanilla essence (extract)
2½ oz. (⅔ cup) plain (all-purpose) flour
7 oz. (⅞ cup) butter
10 oz. (1½ cups) icing (confectioners')
  sugar, sifted
6 standard eggs, separated
4 tablespoons (5 T) ground almonds
Apricot jam (preserves)
3 dessertspoons (3 T) warm coffee

Pre-heat oven to moderate (350°F, Gas Mark 4). Brush an 8 in. round cake tin (pan) with melted butter. Line the base and sides with greaseproof (waxed) paper and brush with more butter.
Break up 6 oz. (6 squares) chocolate and put, with coffee and vanilla essence (extract), into a bowl standing over a pan of hot water. Leave until melted, stirring once or twice, then set aside to cool.
Sift the flour 3 times.
Beat the butter until soft then gradually beat in one-third of the sugar. Continue beating until light and fluffy. Beat in the egg yolks, almonds and cooled chocolate.
Beat the egg whites until stiff, then gradually beat in another third of the sugar. Using a large metal spoon, fold into the chocolate mixture alternately with the flour.
When evenly combined, transfer to the prepared tin (pan) and bake in the centre of the oven for about 1 hour or until a cocktail stick etc. inserted into the centre comes out clean. (Owing to its richness, this cake will not rise very much.) Leave in the tin (pan) for 15 minutes then turn out and cool on a wire (cake) rack.
When completely cold, cut in half horizontally and sandwich together with apricot jam (preserves). Melt a little more apricot jam (preserves) over a low heat and brush over the top and sides of the cake.
To make icing: melt the remaining chocolate and warm coffee over a basin or pan of hot water. Gradually stir in the remaining sugar to form a thickish icing (if too thick, thin down with a

little water or coffee).

Spread over the top and sides of the cake and leave until set before cutting. Accompany each portion with a heaped dessertspoon (spoonful) softly whipped cream if desired.

Apricot Tart – France

8 oz. (2 cups) plain (all-purpose) flour
1½ oz. (4 T) icing (confectioners') sugar
4 oz. (½ cup) butter
2 egg yolks
About 1 tablespoon (1¼ T) milk
1 egg white

Cream filling and topping
1 egg
2 level tablespoons (2½ T) castor (granulated) sugar
1 level tablespoon (1¼ T) plain (all-purpose) flour
1 teaspoon vanilla essence (extract)
¼ pint (⅝ cup) milk
1 large can apricot halves, well-drained
2 level dessertspoons (3 T) apricot jam (preserves)
1 dessertspoon (1 T) water

Sift the flour and sugar into a bowl. Cut in the butter with a pastry cutter or round-topped knife then rub into the dry ingredients finely with fingertips. Mix to a firm paste with the egg yolks and milk. Knead lightly until smooth then wrap and refrigerate for at least 30 minutes.

Pre-heat oven to moderately hot (400°F, Gas Mark 6).

Turn the pastry on to a work surface dusted with flour and roll out to an oblong, approximately 13 × 7½ in. Cut two ¾ in. wide strips from the long sides and brush with egg white. Put back on top of the oblong, along both cut edges, to form a raised border. Press gently to seal, then carefully flake the edges by tapping with the back of a knife.

Place on a baking tray (cookie sheet). Prick the base lightly with a fork, brush the borders with egg white, then bake towards the top of the oven for 15–20 minutes or until pale gold. Cool on a wire (cake) rack.

To make cream filling: whisk the egg and sugar over a basin of hot water until thick and white. Fold in the flour and essence (extract), then gradually stir in the milk. Pour into a pan and heat slowly, stirring, until the mixture boils. Remove from heat and cool.

When completely cold, spread thickly over the pastry base. Arrange rows of apricot halves over the filling then brush with glaze, made by heating the jam (preserves) with the water, straining and re-heating until liquid just begins to boil.

Apricot tart

Cakes for special occasions

In everyone's life, in every family, there is always an occasion that is extra special, be it an engagement, wedding, christening, birthday or even a home coming. As well as the traditional Christmas and Easter cakes, I have included recipes in this section for almost every type of conventional celebration with, in nearly all cases, illustrations to go with them.

I hope every ambitious and enthusiastic cook will find something here to suit the occasion – whatever it may be – and that she will take pride and pleasure in trying out some of the recipes, all of which can be made without too much effort and – just as important these days – expense.

Engagement Cake

4 oz. (1 cup) self-raising flour, sifted
1 level teaspoon baking powder, sifted
4 oz. ($\frac{1}{2}$ cup) luxury or easy-cream
**   margarine**
4 oz. ($\frac{1}{2}$ cup) castor (granulated) sugar
2 large eggs
Finely grated peel of 1 small orange

Chocolate Icing
1 oz. (2 T) luxury or easy-cream
**   margarine**
3 tablespoons ($3\frac{3}{4}$ T) cold water
2 oz. (2 squares) plain (bitter) chocolate
6 oz. (1 cup) icing (confectioners') sugar,
**   sifted**

Decoration
1$\frac{1}{2}$ yd. ribbon (colour to taste)
A circlet of fresh or artificial blossom

Pre-heat oven to moderate (350°F, Gas Mark 4). Brush an 8 in. sandwich tin (cake pan) with melted margarine and line the base with greased greaseproof (waxed) paper.
Place all cake ingredients into a mixing bowl and beat together with a wooden spoon until well-mixed, about 3 minutes.
Transfer to the prepared tin (pan) and bake in the centre of the oven for 25–35 minutes or until well risen and golden. Leave in the tin (pan) for 5 minutes then turn out and cool on a wire (cake) rack.

To make icing and decorate the cake:
Put all the ingredients, except sugar, in a bowl over a saucepan of hot water. Stir until the chocolate is melted and the mixture thickens slightly. Cool a little then beat in the sugar. Continue beating until the icing is of a coating consistency. Pour over the cake and leave to set. Place the cake on a cakeboard or flat plate, tie ribbon round the sides (finishing with a bow), then stand a circlet of blossom on top.

Engagement cake

Wedding Cake

1 lb. (4 cups) plain (all-purpose) flour
2 level teaspoons mixed spice
1 level teaspoon cinnamon
12 oz. (1½ cups) butter or margarine
12 oz. (1½ cups) soft brown sugar
6 standard eggs
2 tablespoons (2½ T) treacle (dark molasses)
4 tablespoons (5 T) sweet sherry or brandy
1 teaspoon almond essence (extract)
1 tablespoon (1¼ T) liquid coffee essence (strong coffee)
2 oz. (½ cup) blanched almonds, chopped
2 oz. (¼ cup) ground almonds
1 lb. (3 cups) sultanas (golden raisins)
12 oz. (just under 2½ cups) currants
8 oz. (1½ cups) seedless raisins
2 oz. (4 pieces) preserved ginger, chopped
4 tablespoons (5 T) glacé cherries, halved
2 oz. (½ cup) mixed chopped peel
Finely grated peel of 1 orange

Almond Paste:
1 lb. (2 cups) ground almonds
8 oz. (1 cup) castor (granulated) sugar
1 lb. (2½ cups) icing (confectioners') sugar, sifted
2 standard eggs
2 teaspoons brandy
1 teaspoon vanilla essence (extract)
½ teaspoon almond essence (extract)
Lemon juice
Apricot jam (preserve)

Royal Icing
5 egg whites
Approximately 2 lb. (5 cups) icing (confectioners') sugar, sifted
Blue food colouring
4 drops glycerine

Pre-heat oven to cool (300°F, Gas Mark 2). Brush one 8 in. and one 6 in. square cake tin (pan) with melted fat. Line the base and sides with double thickness greaseproof (waxed) paper and brush with more fat. Sift together the flour, mixed spice and cinnamon.

Cream the butter or margarine and sugar together until light and fluffy then beat in the whole eggs, one at a time, adding a dessertspoon (tablespoon) dry ingredients with each.

Lightly fold in half the flour mixture, then stir in the treacle (molasses), sherry or brandy, almond essence (extract), coffee essence (coffee) and chopped and ground almonds. Thoroughly mix in the fruit, ginger, cherries, mixed peel and orange peel. Using a large metal spoon, stir in the remaining flour, then transfer the mixture to the prepared tins (pans).

Bake the small cake in the centre of the oven and the large cake on shelf below for 2 hours. Reverse position of cakes. Bake the smaller cake for a further 30–45 minutes, the large cake for another 1½–2 hours, or until a cocktail stick etc. inserted into the centre of the cakes comes out clean.

Leave 20 minutes before turning out and cooling on wire (cake) racks. Wrap in aluminium foil when completely cold and leave for at least one week before covering with Almond Paste.

To make Almond Paste:
Mix together the almonds and sugars then form into a fairly stiff paste with the eggs, brandy, essences (extracts) and lemon juice. Turn on to a sugar-dusted surface and knead until smooth, working in a little extra sifted icing (confectioners') sugar if almond paste is on the wet side, or a little extra beaten egg if it is on the dry side. Brush the sides and tops of both cakes with melted and sieved apricot jam (preserves), then very neatly cover the top and sides of the larger cake with two-thirds of the almond paste. Repeat with the smaller cake using remaining almond paste.

Place on boards 2 in. larger all the way round than the cakes, and set both aside for at least a week before covering with Royal Icing. In this way the almond paste will become firm and therefore the almond oil is not as likely to come through and discolour the white icing.

To make Royal Icing:
Lightly beat the egg whites then gradually add the icing (confectioners') sugar, beating thoroughly until a smooth, semi-stiff (but pliable) icing is formed. Stir in sufficient blue food colouring to make the mixture appear very white, then add the glycerine to prevent the icing becoming rock hard, brittle and difficult to cut.

Spread the icing over the top and sides of the cakes, smoothing with a large, flat-bladed knife (spatula) dipped from time to time in hot water and shaken dry. Leave for a few days for icing to harden before decorating.

To decorate and finish cake:
Make up the Royal Icing as above, using about half to three-quarters of the quantity; omit the glycerine and add 2 teaspoons lemon juice.

Pipe the tops and sides of the two cakes as liked with rosettes, lines of trellis, dots, etc.

Decorate with silver horseshoes and cupids, then fix three small pillars on the lower tier using icing to hold them in place.

When completely set and hardened, stand the smaller tier on the pillars and top with any suitable bridal decoration.

Wedding cake

Christening Cake

12 oz. (3 cups) plain (all-purpose) flour
1 level teaspoon baking powder
8 oz. (1 cup) butter or margarine
8 oz. (1 cup) castor (granulated) sugar
4 standard eggs
12 oz. ($2\frac{1}{2}$ cups) *each* currants and sultanas
    (golden raisins)
4 oz. ($\frac{3}{4}$ cup) mixed chopped peel
4 tablespoons (5 T) glacé cherries,
    quartered
2 oz. ($\frac{1}{2}$ cup) almonds, blanched and
    finely chopped
1 tablespoon rose water

Almond Paste

1 lb ($2\frac{1}{2}$ cups) icing (confectioners') sugar,
    sifted
1 lb. (2 cups) ground almonds
1 standard egg, beaten
1 tablespoon ($1\frac{1}{4}$ T) lemon juice
Few drops each almond and vanilla
    essences (extracts)
4 level tablespoons (5 T) apricot jam
    (preserves)

Royal Icing

3 egg whites
$1\frac{1}{4}$ lb. ($3\frac{1}{4}$ cups) icing (confectioners')
    sugar, sifted
3 drops glycerine

Pre-heat oven to cool (300°F, Gas Mark 2). Brush an 8 in. square tin (pan) with melted fat. Line the base and sides with double thickness greaseproof (waxed) paper. Brush with more fat. Sift together the flour and baking powder.

Cream the fat and sugar until light and fluffy, then beat in the whole eggs, one at a time, adding a dessertspoon (tablespoon) flour with each.

Add remaining ingredients and mix thoroughly. Using a large metal spoon, fold in the remaining flour then transfer the mixture to the prepared tin (pan).

Bake in the centre of the oven for 2 hours. Lower the temperature to 275°F, Gas Mark $\frac{1}{2}$, and bake for a further 1–$1\frac{1}{2}$ hours or until a cocktail stick etc. inserted into the centre comes out clean. If the top of the cake appears to be browning too rapidly, cover with a piece of brown paper. Leave for at least 15 minutes before turning out of the tin (pan) to cool on a wire (cake) rack.

Wrap in aluminium foil when completely cold and store in an air-tight container for at least a week before covering with almond paste.

Note: If a round cake is preferred, bake the mixture in a 9 in. round cake tin (pan).

Christening cake

To make Almond Paste:

Mix together the sugar and almonds. Form into a pliable paste with the beaten eggs, lemon juice and essences (extracts). Knead lightly on a sugared surface until smooth and free from cracks. If on the wet side, work in more sifted sugar; if dry, add a little extra beaten egg.

Brush the top and sides of the cake with melted apricot jam (preserves). Cover neatly with almond paste, then put aside in a cool place for 4–7 days for the paste to harden.

To make Royal Icing:

Lightly whisk the egg whites, then gradually add the sugar, beating well until the icing is smooth, very white and stiff enough to form small peaks. Stir in the glycerine to prevent the icing becoming rock hard, brittle and difficult to cut.

Spread the icing thickly over the top and sides of the cake, smoothing it on with a wide-bladed flat knife (spatula) dipped from time to time in hot water and shaken dry. Leave a few days for the icing to harden before decorating.

To pipe:

Make a quarter quantity of Royal Icing, adding 1 teaspoon lemon juice and 1–2 drops glycerine. Stand the cake on a board and, using a star tube and forcing bag, pipe the top and lower edges and the corners with small rosettes of Royal Icing. Spread the board around the cake thinly with icing then tie a blue or pink ribbon around the edge (as shown in the photograph). Finish by placing a small vase of flowers or the traditional stork ornament on top of the cake.

Golden Wedding Cake

10 oz. (2½ cups) self-raising flour
¼ level teaspoon salt
8 oz. (1 cup) butter or margarine, softened
8 oz. (1 cup) castor (granulated) sugar
1 teaspoon vanilla essence (extract)
1 level teaspoon finely grated lemon peel
   (optional)
4 standard eggs
3 tablespoons (3¾ T) milk

Golden Butter Cream
8 oz. (1 cup) butter
1 lb. (2½ cups) icing (confectioners') sugar
3 teaspoons lemon juice
Yellow food colouring
Apricot jam (preserves)

Glace Icing
2 lb. (7 cups) icing (confectioners') sugar
Strained juice of 1 lemon
Warm water

Pre-heat oven to moderate (350°F, Gas Mark 4). Brush one 9 in., one 8 in. and one 7 in. round sandwich tin (cake pan) with melted margarine. Line the bases with rounds of greased, grease-proof (waxed) paper.
Sift together the flour and salt.
Cream the butter or margarine with sugar, vanilla essence and lemon peel until light and fluffy. Beat in the whole eggs, one at a time, adding a tablespoon flour mixture with each. Using a large metal spoon, fold in the remaining flour mixture alternately with the milk.
Transfer to the prepared tins (pans) and bake in the centre and one shelf below centre of the oven for 15 minutes. Reverse the position of the cakes and continue to bake for a further 10–15 minutes or until well risen and golden. Leave in the tins (pans) for 5 minutes then turn out and cool on wire (cake) racks. Peel away the paper.

To make Butter Cream: beat the butter until soft then gradually beat in the sugar and lemon juice. Continue beating until light and fluffy. Heighten colour by beating in the colouring.
Split each cake in half horizontally and sandwich together with apricot jam (preserves) and a little butter cream. Stand the cakes one on top of the other (largest at the base) and hold in position with a little butter cream. Put on a large rack.

To make glace icing: sift the sugar into a large bowl and gradually mix to a smooth, semi-stiff icing with lemon juice and water. Pour over the top of the tiered cake and allow it to fall down the sides and find its own level; any thin patches should, however, be covered with icing by spreading it on with a knife (spatula).
When the icing has set firmly, carefully transfer the cake to a silver board and pipe lines of butter cream along the lower edge of the bottom cake and also where the tiers join. Decorate with yellow and gold ornaments, flowers, etc.

Silver Wedding Cake

Make exactly as Golden Wedding Cake, but colour the butter cream pale blue with food colouring. Decorate with silver ornaments.

Marshmallow Petal Birthday Cake

Make up Chocolate Sandwich Cake (see page 25). When cold, cut each cake in half horizontally (4 slices).
Make up butter cream: cream 8 oz. (1 cup) butter with 1 lb. (just over 2½ cups) sifted icing (confectioners') sugar and 2 tablespoons (2½ T) milk. Colour pale pink with red food colouring then sandwich layers of cake together generously with butter cream. Swirl remaining cream over top. To make marshmallow petals: snip as many white marshmallows as required 6 times with scissors dipped into hot water (6 petals). Stand on top of cake then place a candle and holder in centre of each.

Valentine Cake

Make up Victoria Sandwich mixture (see page 24).
Bake in a greased and lined heart-shaped tin (pan) or 8 in. sandwich tin (cake pan) for 35–40 minutes in the centre of a moderate oven (350°F, Gas Mark 4).
Leave in the tin (pan) for 5 minutes then turn out on to a wire (cake) rack. Peel away paper. If the cake was baked in a heart-shaped tin (pan) cut in half horizontally. If baked in a sandwich tin (pan), cut into a heart-shape and then slice in half horizontally.
Sandwich the cake together with a little apricot jam (preserves).
Topping: beat ¼ pint (⅝ cup) double cream (whipping cream) with 1 tablespoon (1¼ T) milk until thick, then stir in 2 tablespoons (2½ T) melted and sieved apricot jam (preserves). Spread thickly over the top of the cake.
Break up 3 oz. (3 squares) plain (semi-sweet) chocolate and put into a bowl over hot water. Leave until melted then stir in 1½ oz. (1 cup) cornflakes. Leave until almost cold then pile on top of the cake. Refrigerate for 10–15 minutes for chocolate to harden.
If possible, make and eat on the same day.

Autumn Birthday or Anniversary Cake

4 oz. (1 cup) self-raising flour, sifted
1 level teaspoon baking powder, sifted
4 oz. ($\frac{1}{2}$ cup) easy-cream margarine
4 oz. ($\frac{1}{2}$ cup) castor (granulated) sugar
2 large eggs

Chocolate Glace Fudge Icing

1 oz. (2 T) margarine
3 tablespoons ($3\frac{3}{4}$ T) water
2 oz. (2 squares) plain (bitter) chocolate
6 oz. (1 cup) icing (confectioners') sugar, sifted
2 oz. ($\frac{1}{2}$ cup) blanched and chopped almonds

White Glace Icing

4 level tablespoons (5 T) sifted icing (confectioners') sugar
Few drops warm water

Pre-heat oven to moderate (350°F, Gas Mark 4). Brush an 8 in. sandwich tin (cake pan) with melted margarine and line the base with greased greaseproof (waxed) paper.

Place all cake ingredients into a bowl and beat with a wooden spoon until well mixed, about 3 minutes.

Transfer the mixture to the prepared tin (pan) and bake in the centre of the oven for 25–35 minutes or until well-risen, golden and firm. Leave in the tin (pan) for 5 minutes then turn out and cool on a wire (cake) rack. Place a leaf-shaped paper pattern on top of the cold cake and cut round to form a large leaf.

Chocolate Glacé Fudge Icing: place the margarine, water and chocolate in a bowl standing over a saucepan of hot water. Leave until the chocolate has melted, stirring once or twice. Remove from heat, cool slightly, then beat in the sugar. Continue beating until the mixture is a coating consistency.

Pour over the cake and press the chopped almonds around the sides. Transfer to a cake board.

Sandwich the biscuits together with the butter cream and stand on a board horizontally. Cover all but one end completely with remaining butter cream and ridge with a fork (as shown in photograph). Put the chocolate finger biscuit at the covered end for the tail, then decorate the uncovered 'face' of Dougal with 2 chocolate button eyes and a ½ glacé cherry nose, holding them in position with reserved butter cream. Put 2 small blobs of white butter cream in the centres of chocolate buttons to represent the eyeballs.

Party Cup Cakes

Make up any recipe for Cup Cakes (see rubbing-in and creaming sections, pages 12 and 26). When completely cold, spread each cake with glacé icing: sift about 6 oz. (1 cup) icing (confectioners') sugar into a bowl and mix to a thick icing with a few teaspoons warm water. When the icing has set, pipe the guests' names using a writing tube and melted chocolate.

Catherine Wheel Birthday Cake

1 baked Madeira Cake (see page 26) or
    three 7 in. baked Victoria Sandwich
    cakes (see page 24)
12 oz. (1½ cups) butter
1 lb. (just over 3 cups) icing
    (confectioners') sugar, sifted
1 teaspoon vanilla essence (extract)
½ level tablespoon cocoa powder
Boiling water
Candle holders and candles as required

If using Madeira Cake, cut into 3 pieces horizontally. (If the top has domes, remove with a sharp knife.)
To make butter cream: beat the butter until soft then gradually beat in the sugar and vanilla essence (extract). Divide into 2 portions.
Mix the cocoa powder to smooth paste with boiling water, leave until cold then gradually beat into one portion of butter cream.
Sandwich slices of cake, or sandwich cakes, together using plain butter cream for one layer and chocolate butter cream for the other. Stand the cake on a board.
Put 2 star-shaped tubes into 2 icing (pastry) bags filled with both butter creams. Pipe rosettes, in rings, round the top and sides of the cake, alternating the two-colour butter creams. Chill slightly.
Just before serving, insert candles and holders at an angle to represent a Catherine wheel (as shown in photograph, page 101).

White Glacé Icing: mix the sugar to a stiffish paste with warm water. With a writing tube and forcing bag, pipe lines on the cake to represent the veins of the leaf.

Dougal Cake

8 oz. (1 cup) butter
12 oz. (2 cups) icing (confectioners')
    sugar, sifted
2 level tablespoons (2½ T) cocoa powder
Boiling water
1 teaspoon vanilla essence (extract)
About 24 ginger biscuits (snaps) or Jaffa
    cakes
1 chocolate finger biscuit for tail
2 chocolate buttons for eyes
½ glacé cherry for nose

Beat the butter until soft then gradually beat in the sugar. Continue beating until light and fluffy. Reserve about ½ teaspoon.
Mix the cocoa powder to a smooth paste with water and leave until cold. Beat into the butter cream with the vanilla essence (extract).

Welcome home cake

Welcome Home Cake

4 oz. (1 cup) self-raising flour, sifted
1 level teaspoon baking powder, sifted
4 oz. ($\frac{1}{2}$ cup) luxury or easy-cream
   margarine
4 oz. ($\frac{1}{2}$ cup) castor (granulated) sugar
2 large eggs

Chocolate Icing
3 oz. (6 T) margarine
8 oz. ($1\frac{1}{2}$ cups) icing (confectioners')
   sugar, sifted
1 heaped tablespoon (2 T) cocoa powder,
   blended with 2 tablespoons ($2\frac{1}{2}$ T)
   boiling water

Glace Icing
4 oz. ($\frac{3}{4}$ cup) icing (confectioners') sugar,
   sifted

Few teaspoons water
2 oz. ($\frac{1}{2}$ cup) chopped walnuts

Pre-heat oven to warm (325°F, Gas Mark 3). Well grease and paper-line a heart-shaped tin (pan).
Place all the cake ingredients into a bowl and beat together with a wooden spoon until well-mixed, about 3 minutes.
Transfer the mixture to the prepared tin (pan) and bake in the centre of the oven for 35–40 minutes. Leave in the tin (pan) for 5 minutes then turn out and cool on a wire (cake) rack. Peel away the paper and leave the cake until cold.
Chocolate Icing: place all the ingredients in a bowl and beat together with a wooden spoon until smooth.
Glace Icing: place the sugar and water in a bowl and beat together with a wooden spoon for 1–2 minutes.
To assemble cake: cut the cake horizontally into

92

3 layers then sandwich together with some of the chocolate icing.

Cover the top of the cake with the glacé icing and when completely set, spread a little of the remaining chocolate icing around the sides.

Press the walnuts round the sides and, with the remaining chocolate icing, pipe 'Welcome Home' on top of the cake, and lines of rosettes around top and lower edges.

Soldier Birthday Cake

Make up Victoria Sandwich mixture (see page 24) and bake in a 7 in. very well greased ring tin (spring-form pan) in the centre of a warm oven (325°F, Gas Mark 3) for about 45–55 minutes. Leave in the tin (pan) for 5 minutes then turn out on to a wire (cake) rack. Leave until completely cold.

To make icing: sift 12 oz. (2 cups) icing (confectioners') sugar into a bowl and mix to a thickish icing with a little warm water, adding it teaspoon by teaspoon. Pour over the cake, allowing it to run down the sides and find its own level.

When the icing has completely set, transfer the cake to a serving plate and stand a small dish on top. Fill the dish and surround the base with sugar-coated chocolate drops. Stand any appropriate children's toy beside the cake.

Easter Flake Cake

Make a Madeira Cake (see page 26).

When completely cold, cut twice horizontally (3 slices).

Make vanilla butter cream: beat 8 oz. (1 cup) softened butter with 12 oz. (2 cups) sifted icing (confectioners') sugar and 1 teaspoon vanilla essence (extract). Continue beating until light and fluffy. Sandwich the cake together liberally with butter cream, then spread remainder thickly over the top and sides. Coat completely with about 6 large, crushed milk chocolate flake bars. Put a few fondant Easter eggs in the centre then stand a couple of fluffy chicks nearby.

Shortcut Simnel Cake

Almond paste
1 lb. (2 cups) ground almonds
1 lb. (2½ cups) icing
    (confectioners') sugar, sifted
½ teaspoon *each* vanilla and almond
    essence (extract)
3 teaspoons lemon juice
2 egg yolks (reserve 1 egg white)

Cake
6 oz. (1½ cups) self-raising flour

Dash of salt
½ level teaspoon nutmeg
¼ level teaspoon ground ginger
1 teaspoon *each* mixed spice and
    cinnamon
6 oz. (¾ cup) butter or margarine
6 oz. (¾ cup) soft brown sugar
3 standard eggs
8 oz. (1½ cups) mixed (chopped) dried
    fruit
Apricot jam (preserves)

To make almond paste: mix the almonds and sugar well together then bind to a stiffish paste with the essences (extracts), lemon juice and egg yolks. If it is on the wet side, work in a little extra sifted icing (confectioners') sugar; if dry, add a little more lemon juice.

Divide into 3 equal pieces. Dust a work surface with sifted icing (confectioners') sugar or castor (granulated) sugar and roll 2 of the pieces into 8 in. rounds.

To make the cake: pre-heat oven to warm (325°F, Gas Mark 3). Brush two 8 in. sandwich tins (cake pans) with melted fat. Line the bases and sides with greaseproof (waxed) paper then brush with more fat.

Sift the flour, salt and spices into a bowl.

Cream the butter or margarine with the sugar until light and fluffy then beat in the whole eggs, one at a time, adding a tablespoon sifted dry ingredients with each.

Stir in the fruit then gradually fold in remaining dry ingredients with a large metal spoon. Divide equally between the prepared tins (pans). Bake in the centre of the oven for about 45 minutes until well risen and golden, or until a cocktail stick comes out clean from the centre.

Leave in the tins (pans) for 10 minutes then turn out and cool on a wire (cake) rack. Peel away the paper, spread thinly with apricot jam (preserves) and leave until cold.

Sandwich the cakes together with one round of marzipan (almond paste). Brush the top of the cake with more jam (preserves) and cover with second portion of almond paste. Form the remaining paste into 12 balls and stand round the edge of the cake. Brush with lightly beaten reserved egg white and either stand cake under the grill or put in a very hot oven (450°F, Gas Mark 8) for a few minutes to glaze the top.

If liked, fill the centre with glacé icing made by mixing a little sifted icing (confectioners') sugar to a thickish paste with a little warm water. Stand a fluffy chick on top when the icing has set. Tie a wide band of ribbon (backed with greaseproof (waxed) paper) round the cake, finishing with a large bow.

Mince Pies with Corn Oil Pastry

3½ fl. oz. (7 T) corn oil
3½ fl. oz. (7 T) cold water
8 oz. (2 cups) plain (all-purpose) flour
¼ level teaspoon salt
¾–1 lb. (1½–2 cups) mincemeat
Castor (granulated) sugar

Pre-heat oven to moderately hot (375°F, Gas Mark 5). Well grease 12 deep bun tins (muffin cups).
Pour the oil and water into a bowl. Beat for about 30 seconds to form an emulsion, then sift in the flour and salt. Using a fork, mix to a firm dough then knead quickly and lightly until smooth.
Sandwich between 2 sheets of oiled greaseproof (waxed) paper and roll out evenly, or roll out on a well floured surface. Cut out 12 rounds with a 2½–3 in. biscuit cutter and use to line the prepared bun tins (muffin cups). Fill with equal amounts of mincemeat and moisten the pastry edges with water.
Cut out slightly smaller round for the tops and remove the centres with a small biscuit cutter or bottle top. Stand on top of the pies and pinch the pastry case edges and lids well together to seal. Bake near the top of the oven for about 20–25 minutes. Cool to lukewarm, then turn out of the tins (cups) and dredge with castor (granulated) sugar.

Traditional Mince Pies

8 oz. (2 cups) plain (all-purpose) flour
Dash of salt
4 oz. (½ cup) mixture of margarine and white cooking fat (shortening)
About 3 tablespoons (3¾ T) water to mix
¾–1 lb. (1½–2 cups) mincemeat
A little beaten egg for brushing
Icing (confectioners') sugar

Pre-heat oven to hot (425°F, Gas Mark 7). Lightly grease 12 deep bun tins (muffin cups).
Sift the flour and salt into a bowl. Add the fat and cut into the dry ingredients with a pastry cutter or round-topped knife (spatula), then rub in lightly with fingertips. Mix to a stiff dough with water and knead lightly until smooth. Roll out evenly then proceed as in previous recipe.
Brush the tops with beaten egg then bake for about 20 minutes just above the centre of a moderately hot oven (400°F, Gas Mark 6).
Remove from the tins (cups) when lukewarm and sift icing (confectioners') sugar over the tops.

Christmas Star Pie

Pastry

Shortcrust as given for Traditional Mince Pies

Filling

1 large cooking apple, peeled and finely grated
12 oz. (1½ cups) mincemeat

Christmas star pie

Pre-heat oven to hot (425°F, Gas Mark 7). Well grease a 9 in. heat-proof pie plate.

Turn the pastry out on to a lightly floured surface, knead quickly until smooth then divide in two. Roll out one half into a round and use to line the prepared plate. Fill with a layer of grated apples topped with mincemeat, then moisten pastry edges with water.

Roll out the remaining pastry into a 10 in. round and cut out a ring of 8 stars about 2 in. in from the outside edge.

Place the lid carefully over the filling and seal firmly by pressing the edges well together. Arrange the pastry stars around the outer edge, holding them in place with a little water.

Bake towards the top of the oven for 25 minutes, then reduce temperature to moderate (350°F, Gas Mark 4) and bake for a further 15–20 minutes. Dust with sifted icing (confectioners') sugar and serve warm with cream.

Yule log

Yule Log

Cake

1 jam-filled Swiss roll (jelly roll), bought or home-made (see page 50).

Chocolate Butter Cream

3 oz. (6 T) butter, softened
6 oz. (1 cup) icing (confectioners') sugar, sifted
$\frac{1}{2}$ teaspoon vanilla essence (extract)
1 tablespoon ($1\frac{1}{4}$ T) warm milk
3 level tablespoons ($3\frac{3}{4}$ T) cocoa powder, sifted
A little extra icing (confectioners') sugar

Cream the butter and sugar together until light and fluffy, then beat in the vanilla essence (extract) and milk. Reserve 1 rounded tablespoon for decoration. Add the cocoa to remainder and beat in thoroughly until the butter cream is smooth and all the ingredients well blended.
Cut a $1\frac{1}{2}$ in. diagonal slice off one end of the Swiss roll (jelly roll) to represent a small log. Put on top of the Swiss roll (jelly roll), a third of the way along, holding in place with butter cream.
Cover the ends of the large and small 'logs' with reserved plain butter cream and, using a writing pipe and forcing bag, decorate with rings of chocolate butter cream.
Cover the 'log' all over with chocolate butter cream and ridge with a fork for a roughened effect. Shower with 'snow' using icing (confectioners') sugar and decorate with robins and sprigs of holly.

Christmas Cake made with corn oil

2 standard eggs
6 oz. ($\frac{3}{4}$ cup) soft brown sugar
$\frac{1}{4}$ pint ($\frac{5}{8}$ cup) corn oil
10 oz. ($2\frac{1}{2}$ cups) plain (all-purpose) flour
$1\frac{1}{2}$ level teaspoons baking powder
Dash of salt
3 tablespoons sweet sherry or port
1 lb. 6 oz. ($4\frac{1}{2}$ cups) mixed (chopped) dried fruit
4 oz. (just under 1 cup) mixed chopped peel
3 oz. ($\frac{3}{4}$ cup) blanched and chopped almonds
3 tablespoons ($3\frac{3}{4}$ T) glacé cherries, chopped

Almond Paste

12 oz. ($1\frac{1}{2}$ cups) ground almonds
6 oz. (1 cup) icing (confectioners') sugar, sifted
1 standard egg, beaten
$\frac{1}{4}$ level teaspoon *each* almond and vanilla essence (extract)
A little lemon juice

Royal Icing

$1\frac{1}{2}$ lb. (4 cups) icing (confectioners') sugar, sifted
3 standard egg whites
2 teaspoons fresh lemon juice
1 teaspoon glycerine

Pre-heat oven to cool (300°F, Gas Mark 2). Brush an 8 in. round or 7 in. square cake tin (pan) with melted fat. Line the base and sides with greaseproof (waxed) paper and brush with more fat.
Beat together the eggs, sugar and oil. Stir in flour sifted with the baking powder and salt. Add the sherry or port. Fold in the fruit, peel, almonds and cherries. Transfer to the prepared tin (pan) and level the top with a knife.
Bake in the centre of the oven for $2\frac{1}{2}$–3 hours or until a cocktail stick, inserted into the centre comes out clean. Leave in the tin (pan) for at least 15 minutes before turning out on to a wire (cake) rack.
When completely cold, wrap in foil and leave for at least a week to mature before covering with almond paste.
To make Almond Paste: see All-In-One Christmas Cake (page 99), then use to cover the top

Christmas cake made with corn oil (above right)
Golden wedding cake (below right)

All-in-one Christmas or Birthday cake
1 : Brushing cake with jam (preserves)

2 : Covering sides of cake with strip of almond paste

3 : Bringing edges together

4 : Smoothing icing round sides

5 : Piping on decorations

6 : Finished cake

and sides of the cake.

To ice: make up Royal Icing as directed in All-In-One Christmas Cake (recipe below), beating in the lemon juice and glycerine at the end. Stand the cake on a board, securing it with a little icing, then cover the top and sides thickly with about three-quarters of the icing. For a snow effect, press the back of a teaspoon into the icing and lift up so that small peaks form.

If liked, smooth the middle of cake with a knife dipped in hot water, then pipe a border of rosettes round the smooth portion. Repeat round lower edge.

Decorate with ribbon and Christmas ornaments.

All-in-one Christmas or Birthday Cake

8 oz. (1 cup) luxury or easy-cream margarine
8 oz. (1 cup) soft brown sugar
5 standard eggs
Finely grated peel of 1 lemon
4 oz. ($\frac{3}{4}$ cup) mixed chopped peel
2 oz. ($\frac{1}{2}$ cup) almonds, blanched and chopped
2 oz. ($\frac{1}{4}$ cup) ground almonds
2 tablespoons ($2\frac{1}{2}$ T) brandy (optional)
1 tablespoon ($1\frac{1}{4}$ T) black treacle (dark molasses)
$1\frac{1}{2}$ lb. (5 cups) mixed (chopped) dried fruit
4 tablespoons (5 T) glacé cherries, quartered
9 oz. ($2\frac{1}{4}$ cups) plain (all-purpose) flour, sifted
2 level teaspoons baking powder, sifted
1 level teaspoon nutmeg, sifted
1 level teaspoon mixed spice, sifted

Almond Paste
1 lb. (2 cups) ground almonds
8 oz. ($1\frac{1}{2}$ cups) icing (confectioners') sugar
8 oz. (1 cup) castor (granulated) sugar
$1\frac{1}{2}$ teaspoons lemon juice
3 drops almond essence (extract)
1 large egg
Apricot jam (preserves) for brushing

Royal Icing
4 standard egg whites
2 lb. (5 cups) icing (confectioners') sugar, sifted
2 teaspoons glycerine (to prevent icing from becoming over-brittle)

Pre-heat oven to very cool (275°F, Gas Mark $\frac{1}{2}$). Brush a 9 in. round or 8 in. square cake tin (pan) with melted fat. Line the base and sides with double thickness greased greaseproof (waxed) paper and brush with more fat. Tie a strip of folded brown paper round the outside of the tin to prevent the outer edges of the cake burning.

Place all the cake ingredients in a large mixing bowl and beat together with a wooden spoon until very well mixed, 4–5 minutes.

Transfer the mixture to the prepared tin (pan) and smooth the top with a knife. Stand on a baking tray (sheet) covered with thick paper and bake in the centre of the oven for $4\frac{1}{2}$–5 hours. Leave in the tin (pan) for 15–20 minutes then turn out and cool on a wire rack.

When completely cold, wrap in foil and store in an air-tight container for a minimum of one week to mature before covering with Almond Paste.

To make Almond Paste: place all the ingredients in a bowl and mix well together to form a stiff paste; knead until smooth. Dust a work top with castor (granulated) sugar and roll out one-third of the paste to a round large enough to cover the top of the cake. Brush the cake with apricot jam (preserves) and cover with Almond Paste. Trim the edges. Roll out remaining two-thirds of Almond Paste into a long strip the length and width of the sides of the cake. Brush the sides with apricot jam (preserves) and cover with Almond Paste. Seal the join.

Allow Almond Paste to dry for at least 3–4 days before icing.

To make icing: whisk the egg whites until frothy. Add the sifted sugar a little at a time, beating well until the icing stands up in peaks when the beaters are lifted out of the bowl. Beat in the glycerine. Cover with a damp cloth to prevent the icing hardening.

To ice and decorate: transfer the cake to a board, holding it in place with a little Royal Icing. Spread about two-thirds of the icing smoothly over the top and sides of the cake, using a large, flat-bladed knife (spatula) or piece of plastic dipped in hot water. Leave until the icing has dried before decorating. Keep left-over icing covered with a damp cloth.

To pipe: fill a large icing (pastry) bag, fitted with a star-shaped tube, with the remaining icing and pipe a scalloped border round the top and lower edges.

If liked, colour any remaining icing green or red and, with writing tube, outline a Christmas card and greeting on top of the cake.

Finish with a sprig of holly and silver balls. A length of ribbon may be tied into a bow round the sides of the cake if desired.

Easter flake cake (top left)
Traditional mince pies (top right)
Marshmallow petal birthday cake (bottom right)
and Party cup cakes (front left)
Dougal cake (opposite above)
Catherine wheel birthday cake (opposite below)

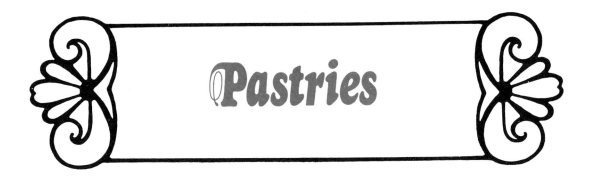

Pastries

The sort of delectable – in some cases ornamental – pastries and tarts which one sees and admires in the windows of luxury patisserie shops do require special skills and expertize to make as they should be made. Many of them are far too tricky and time-consuming to reproduce satisfactorily, and therefore in this section I have included only those recipes for pastries which I know from experience can be made by any competent cook.

Meringues

2 large egg whites
Dash of cream of tartar of a squeeze of
   lemon juice
5 oz. (10 T) castor (granulated) sugar
2 level teaspoons cornflour (cornstarch)
$\frac{1}{4}$ pint ($\frac{5}{8}$ cup) double cream (whipping
   cream)

Pre-heat oven to very cool (225°F, Gas Mark $\frac{1}{4}$).
Brush a large baking tray (sheet) with oil then line with piece of greaseproof (waxed) paper. *Do not oil the paper.*
Put the egg whites and cream of tartar or lemon juice into a large, clean, dry bowl. Beat until stiff.
Gradually beat in half the sugar and continue beating until the meringue is shiny and stands in firm peaks when the beaters are lifted out of the bowl.
Gently beat in half the remaining sugar and cornflour (cornstarch), then *fold* in the remaining sugar.
With a large meringue tube and icing bag, pipe 16 whirls on to the prepared tray (sheet). Put into the lower part of the oven and bake for about 1½ hours; they should have turned from white to the palest cream colour.
Carefully remove the paper, turn the meringues upside down and return to oven for a further 30 minutes to dry out completely.
Transfer to a wire (cake) rack and store in an air-tight container when cold.
Before serving, sandwich meringues together with the cream, beaten until thick.
Note: Meringues will keep indefinitely in an air-tight container, so always fill with cream immediately before serving – never in advance. Instead of piping meringues, they may be spooned on to the tray (sheet) with a dessert-spoon (tablespoon) dipped in hot water.

Almond Triangles

8 oz. (2 cups) self-raising flour
1 level teaspoon cinnamon
$\frac{1}{2}$ level teaspoon *each* mixed spice and
   ground ginger
5 oz. (10 T) butter
3 oz. (6 T) soft brown sugar (dark variety)
2 oz. ($\frac{1}{2}$ cup) blanched and lightly toasted
   almonds, cut into slivers
Yolks of 2 standard eggs
Milk
Apricot jam (preserves)
1 standard egg white

Pre-heat oven to moderately hot (375°F, Gas Mark 5).
Sift the flour and spices into bowl. Add the butter and cut into the dry ingredients with a pastry cutter or round-topped knife, then rub in finely with fingertips. Add the sugar and almonds, then mix to a stiff but pliable dough with the egg yolks and milk as necessary.
Knead lightly until smooth. Divide into 2 equal-sized pieces and roll each out into an 8 in. square. Put on to a lightly greased baking tray (cookie sheet), spread (but not too thickly) with apricot jam (preserves) and cover with the other square of pastry. Beat the egg white to a froth then brush over the top.
Bake just above the centre of the oven for about 30–40 minutes or until golden brown. Leave until almost cold then cut into triangles.
Store in an air-tight container when cold.

Almond triangles (left)
Almond tarts (above)
Chocolate boxes (below)

Orange and grape flan
1 : Lining flan case with pastry

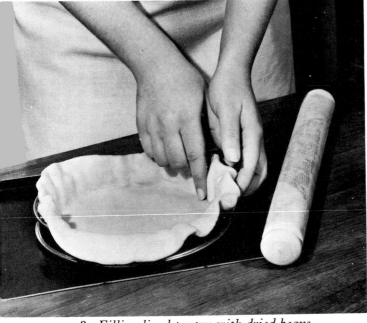

2 : Trimming off surplus pastry with rolling pin

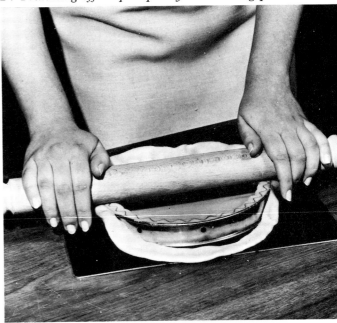

3 : Filling lined pastry with dried beans

4 : Fruit being prepared to go into filled flan

5 : Oranges being segmented

6 : Prepared fruit being arranged in flan

Orange and Grape Flan

6 oz. shortcrust pastry made with 6 oz.
    (1½ cups) flour and 3 oz. (6 T) fat etc., or
    1 large packet frozen shortcrust pastry,
    thawed

Filling
1 level tablespoon (1¼ T) custard powder
    (cornstarch)
2 level tablespoons (2½ T) sugar
¼ pint (⅝ cup) milk
¼ pint (⅝ cup) double cream (whipping
    cream)
2 medium oranges
8 black grapes

Glaze
4 tablespoons (5 T) marmalade (orange
    preserves)
2 tablespoons (2½ T) water

Pre-heat oven to moderately hot (400°F, Gas
Mark 6). Stand an 8 in. fluted flan ring on a
lightly greased baking tray (sheet).
Roll out the pastry into a 10 in. circle and use to
line the flan ring. Line the inside of the pastry
with greaseproof (waxed) paper and fill with
dried beans. (This prevents the pastry rising as
it cooks, but as a speedy alternative simply prick
the pastry lightly with a fork and line with foil —
beans are then unnecessary.)
Bake just above the centre of the oven for 15
minutes. Remove the paper and beans or foil
and return the pastry case to the oven for a
further 10–15 minutes or until pale gold.
Remove from the oven, leave for 5 minutes, then
carefully lift off the flan ring and leave until
completely cold.

To make filling:
Put the custard powder (cornstarch) and sugar
into a saucepan. Gradually mix to a smooth

7 : Finished flan

liquid with the milk. Slowly bring to the boil,
stirring continuously. Cover with damp greaseproof (waxed) paper (when paper is removed
skin comes away with it) and leave until cold.
Beat the cream until softly stiff, then fold into
the custard with the finely grated peel of 1
orange. Spoon the mixture into the flan case.
Cut the grapes in half and remove the pips
(seeds). Remove the peel and pith from the
oranges with a sharp knife. Remove the orange
segments by cutting with a sharp knife between
the membranes.
Arrange the grapes round the outside edge of the
flan and the orange segments inside. Place one
grape in the centre.
For glaze: heat the marmalade (preserves) with
the water, strain, then brush over the fruit.
Note: If using cornstarch, include 1 level teaspoon vanilla essence in filling mixture.

Cream Horns

1 large packet frozen puff pastry (or
    home-made using 8 oz. (2 cups) flour)
Beaten egg for brushing
Sugar for dredging
Red jam (preserves)
½ pint (1¼ cups) double cream (whipping
    cream)
1 teaspoon vanilla essence (extract)
3 level teaspoons (1 T) icing
    (confectioners') sugar, sifted
2 tablespoons (2½ T) milk

Grease 12 cream horn tins (forms) with melted
fat. Rinse a large baking tray (sheet) with water
and leave it damp. Roll out the pastry thinly and
cut into 12 long strips, about 1 in. wide. Brush
one side of each strip with cold water. Wind each
strip, with dampened side inside, round the tins
(forms), starting from the pointed end and overlapping the strip slightly so that there are no
gaps. Transfer to the tray (sheet), brush with
egg and sprinkle with sugar. Leave to 'relax'
in a cool place for 30 minutes.
Meanwhile, pre-heat oven to very hot (450°F,
Gas Mark 8).
Bake the cream horns just above the centre of
the oven for 20–25 minutes or until golden
brown and puffy. Remove from the oven and
gently lift on to a wire (cake) rack.
When almost cold, carefully remove the tins
(forms) from the pastry cases. Put a little jam
(preserves) into the pointed end of each pastry
horn then fill with the cream, whipped until
thick with the essence (extract), sifted sugar and
milk.
When in season, decorate each by pressing a
fresh strawberry into the top.

Strawberry tarts

Strawberry tarts

8 oz. shortcrust made with 8 oz. (2 cups)
  flour and 4 oz. ($\frac{1}{2}$ cup) fat, or 1 large
  packet frozen shortcrust pastry, thawed
Filling and Decoration
$\frac{1}{4}$ **pint ($\frac{5}{8}$ cup) whipped cream (whipping**
  cream)
$\frac{3}{4}$**–1 lb. (2–2$\frac{1}{2}$ cups) strawberries, washed**
  and halved
3 level tablespoons (3$\frac{3}{4}$ T) redcurrant jelly
1 dessertspoon (1 T) water

Pre-heat oven to moderately hot (400°F, Gas Mark 6). Well grease 12 deepish bun tins (muffin cups).

Roll out the pastry and cut into 12 rounds with a 3 in. fluted biscuit cutter. Line the tins (cups) with the pastry rounds and either prick all over with a fork, or line with aluminium foil to prevent the pastry rising as it cooks.

Bake near the top of the oven for 20 minutes or until pale gold. Carefully remove from the tins (cups) and cool on a wire (cake) rack. Put a little whipped cream into each tartlet case, then pile high with halved strawberries. Glaze with the redcurrant jelly, heated and melted with the water. Top with a spoonful of cream and a tiny cookie crisp.

Cookie crisps

Knead the pastry trimmings lightly together, roll out evenly and cut into tiny rounds. Brush with egg white, sprinkle with castor (granulated) sugar and bake towards the top of the oven for 5–6 minutes. Cool on a wire (cake) rack.

Chocolate Boxes

8 oz. (8 squares) plain (semi-sweet)
  chocolate
4 oz. (1 cup) self-raising flour
Dash of salt
$\frac{1}{2}$ **level teaspoon baking powder**
4 oz. ($\frac{1}{2}$ cup) easy-cream margarine
4 oz. ($\frac{1}{2}$ cup) castor (granulated) sugar
2 standard eggs

To finish the cakes
4 oz. ($\frac{1}{2}$ cup) granulated sugar
$\frac{1}{4}$ pint ($\frac{5}{8}$ cup) water
1 tablespoon ($1\frac{1}{4}$ T) orange squash (orange soda pop)
4 tablespoons (5 T) strawberry jam (preserves)
6 tablespoons ($7\frac{1}{2}$ T) double cream (whipping cream), whipped
12 whole strawberries

Pre-heat oven to moderately hot (375°F, Gas Mark 5). Well grease and paper line an 11 × 7 in. Swiss roll tin (jelly roll pan).
Break up the chocolate and melt in a bowl over a pan of hot water. Spread on a piece of waxed paper measuring 12 × 9 in. Leave in a cool place to set.
Sift the flour, salt and baking powder into a bowl. Add the remaining cake ingredients and beat thoroughly until well mixed, about 3 minutes. Transfer to the prepared tin (pan) and bake in the centre of the oven for 25–30 minutes then turn out on to a wire (cake) rack. Peel away the paper. Dissolve the sugar in the water, stirring over a low heat. Bring to the boil, boil for 1 minute, add the orange squash (soda) and remove from heat. Cut the cake in half and sandwich together with jam (preserves). Cut off the crusty edges, then pour the syrup over the cake, allowing it to soak in well. Cut into twelve $1\frac{1}{2}$ in. squares.
Melt the remaining jam and brush over the sides of each square. With a sharp knife, cut the chocolate into forty-eight $1\frac{1}{2}$ in. squares and press 4 against the sides of each cake. Spoon or pipe a whirl of cream on top and decorate with a strawberry.

Party Pieces

4 oz. (1 cup) self-raising flour
$\frac{1}{2}$ level teaspoon baking powder
4 oz. ($\frac{1}{2}$ cup) luxury or easy-cream margarine
4 oz. ($\frac{1}{2}$ cup) castor (granulated) sugar
2 standard eggs
Grated peel of 1 small orange or lemon

Icing
8 oz. ($1\frac{1}{3}$ cups) icing (confectioners') sugar, sifted
Strained orange or lemon juice

Decorations
Orange cup cakes
Mimosa balls
Chocolate buttons
Leaves cut from angelica

Lemon cup cakes
Glacé cherries, halved
Leaves cut from angelica
Chocolate drops

Pre-heat oven to moderately hot (400°F, Gas Mark 6). Stand 20 fluted paper cases in 20 ungreased bun tins (muffin cups).
Sift the flour and baking powder into a bowl, then add all remaining cake ingredients. Beat with a wooden spoon until well mixed.
Place a heaped teaspoon of the mixture in the cases. Bake towards the top of the oven for 15–20 minutes. Cool on a wire (cake) rack.
To make icing: sift the sugar into a bowl, then mix to a smooth icing with orange or lemon juice, adding it teaspoon by teaspoon.
To decorate cakes: cover the tops smoothly with icing and leave until set. Add decorations.

Party pieces

Almond Slices

6 oz. shortcrust pastry made with 6 oz.
   (1½ cups) flour and 3 oz. (4 T) fat, or
   part of a large packet of frozen shortcrust pastry, thawed
1 tablespoon (1¼ T) jam (preserves)

Macaroon topping
4 oz. (½ cup) castor (granulated) sugar
4 oz. (¾ cup) icing (confectioners') sugar,
   sifted
4 oz. (½ cup) ground almonds
3 level tablespoons (3¾ T) semolina
1 standard egg + 1 extra white
1 teaspoon almond essence (extract)
2 tablespoons (2½ T) almonds, blanched
   and split

Pre-heat oven to moderately hot (400°F, Gas
Mark 6). Well grease a large baking tray (sheet).
Turn the pastry on to a lightly floured board and
knead until smooth. Roll out into two strips
measuring approximately 12 × 4 in. Transfer
to the prepared tray (sheet) and spread thinly
with jam.
Macaroon topping: mix the dry ingredients
together. Stir in the egg, egg white and essence
(extract). Mix thoroughly then spread over the
pastry. Decorate with split almonds.
Bake in the centre of the oven for 20–25 minutes
or until pale gold.
Cool before cutting into fingers.
Store in an air-tight container when cold.

Exmoor Honey Tarts

6 oz. shortcrust pastry made with 6 oz.
   (1½ cups) flour and 3 oz. (6 T) fat, or
   part of a large packet of frozen
   shortcrust pastry, thawed
12 teaspoons (4 T) clear honey

Almond filling
2 oz. (¼ cup) luxury or easy-cream
   margarine
2 oz. (¼ cup) brown sugar
3 oz. (¾ cup) self-raising flour, sifted
½ teaspoon baking powder, sifted
1 heaped teaspoon (2 teaspoons) bought
   marzipan, chopped
½ teaspoon almond essence (extract)
1 large egg
Sifted icing (confectioners') sugar to
   dredge

Pre-heat oven to moderately hot (375°F, Gas
Mark 5). Well grease 24 small bun tins (muffin
cups).

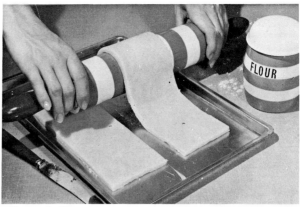

Almond slices
1 : Putting strips of pastry onto baking tray (cookie sheet)

2 : Decorating edges of pastry

*3 : Spreading pastry with topping and
   decorating with almonds*

4 : Finished almond slices

Christmas garland (left)
Danish-style Christmas cake (above)
All-Bran tea bread (below)

Roll out the pastry thinly and cut into rounds with a 2 in. biscuit cutter. Place in the prepared tins (pans), then put $\frac{1}{2}$ teaspoon honey in the base of each.

Almond Filling: place all the ingredients in a bowl and beat together until well mixed, about 3 minutes. Put equal amounts of the mixture in the prepared pastry cases. Bake towards the top of the oven for about 15–20 minutes or until well risen and golden. Cool on a wire (cake) rack. Dredge with sifted sugar before serving.

Chocolate Pineapple Treats

1 cream-filled chocolate Swiss roll (jelly roll)
6 pineapple slices, well-drained
$\frac{1}{4}$ pint ($\frac{5}{8}$ cup) double cream (whipping cream)
Few glacé cherries and strips of angelica

Cut the Swiss roll (jelly roll) into 6 even slices. Arrange on a serving dish. Stand a slice of pineapple on each piece. Whip the cream until thick then pipe a whirl in the centre of each pineapple slice. Decorate with small pieces of cherries and angelica.

Cherry Cream Baskets

4 oz. shortcrust pastry made with 4 oz. (1 cup) flour and 2 oz. (4 T) fat, or 1 small packet frozen shortcrust pastry, thawed
6 teaspoons (2 T) apricot jam (preserves)

Almond Cake Mixture
3 oz. ($\frac{3}{4}$ cup) self-raising flour
2 oz. ($\frac{1}{4}$ cup) butter or margarine
2 oz. ($\frac{1}{4}$ cup) castor (granulated) sugar
1 standard egg
1 oz. (2 T) ground almonds
Almond essence (extract)
Milk to mix
Whipped cream
6 glacé cherries, halved
Strips of angelica

Pre-heat oven to moderately hot (400°F, Gas Mark 6). Well grease 12 deepish bun tins (muffin cups).
Roll out the pastry evenly and cut into 3 in. rounds with a fluted cutter. Use to line the prepared tins (cups).
Put $\frac{1}{2}$ teaspoon jam (preserves) into each, then three-quarters fill with the Almond Cake Mixture.

Chocolate pineapple treats

Sift the flour into a bowl.
Cream the butter or margarine and sugar together until light and fluffy, then beat in the egg, almonds and essence (extract).
Fold in flour alternately with a few teaspoons milk to form a stiffish consistency.
Bake the cakes just above the centre of the oven for 25–30 minutes or until well risen and golden. Turn out and cool on a wire (cake) rack.
When completely cold, cut a slice off the top of each tartlet then cut again into 2 (to give 2 'wings'). Pipe whipped cream over the top of each tartlet then insert the 'wings' at an angle. Finish with half a cherry in the centre of each and a handle shaped from a strip of angelica.

Almond Tarts

Follow recipe as above, but use shallow bun tins (tart pans) instead of deep ones (muffin cups). Fill with ground almond mixture and scatter tops heavily with flaked almonds before baking. When cool, brush the tops with melted apricot jam (preserves) and top with half a cherry.

Cherry cream baskets

Coffee Eclairs

2½ oz. (½ cup) plain (all-purpose) flour
Dash of salt
¼ pint (½ cup) water
2 oz. (3 T) butter or luxury margarine
2 standard eggs, well beaten
½ pint (1¼ cups) double cream (whipping cream)
2 level tablespoons (2½ T) castor (granulated) sugar
2 tablespoons (2½ T) milk

Icing
9 oz. (1½ cups) icing (confectioners') sugar, sifted
3–4 dessertspoons (3 T) very strong coffee

Pre-heat oven to moderately hot (400°F, Gas Mark 6). Well grease a large baking tray (sheet). Sift the flour and salt together twice.
Put the water and butter or margarine in a saucepan. Slowly melt the butter over a gentle heat, then bring the mixture to a rolling boil. Lower the heat and tip in the flour all at once.

Stir briskly until the mixture thickens sufficiently to form a ball in the centre of the pan, leaving the sides clean. Remove from heat and cool slightly.
Very gradually beat in the eggs and continue beating until the mixture is smooth, shiny and stands in soft peaks when lifted with a spoon. Fit a large forcing (pastry) bag with a ½ in. plain

Coffee cream buns

Custard tarts

tube. Fill with the pastry then pipe twelve 4 in. lengths on to the prepared tray (sheet).

Bake in the centre of the oven for 10 minutes.

Reduce the temperature to moderate (350°F, Gas Mark 4) and bake for a further 20–25 minutes or until éclairs are well puffed and golden.

Remove from the oven and make a slit in the side of each.

Using a teaspoon, carefully scoop out any soft dough which may be left inside the éclairs, then return to the oven for a further 5 minutes to dry out. Transfer to a wire cooling (cake) rack.

When completely cold, slice in half lengthwise and fill with the cream, whipped until thick with the sugar and milk.

To make icing: mix the sugar to a smooth icing with the coffee, stirring briskly without beating.

Lift up each éclair and dip the top into the icing. If preferred, spread icing on with a knife.

Coffee Cream Buns

Follow the éclair recipe (above) exactly, but put 16 small mounds of choux pastry (well apart) on to the prepared tray (sheet). When completely cold, halve then fill and ice as for éclairs.

Chocolate Eclairs and Cream Buns

Make exactly as for Coffee Eclairs and Cream Buns (above), but cover with chocolate icing: melt 2 oz. (2 squares) plain (bitter) chocolate with 1 teaspoon butter in a bowl over hot water. Stir in 2 tablespoons (2½ T) warm water and 1 teaspoon vanilla essence (extract). Gradually beat in 4 oz. (just under 1 cup) sifted icing (confectioners') sugar. Leave in the cool to thicken up slightly before using.

Note: Eclairs and cream buns puff up more if the tray on which they are placed is covered with an inverted roasting tin (pan) while they are baking. If the pastry is a pale colour after the required amount of baking time, uncover and return to oven for a further 5–7 minutes.

Custard Tarts

6 oz. shortcrust made with 6 oz. (1½ cups) plain (all-purpose) flour and 3 oz. (6 T) fat, or part of a large packet of frozen shortcrust pastry, thawed
1 egg white
6 level teaspoons fresh white breadcrumbs
1 standard egg + 1 egg yolk
¼ pint (⅝ cup) single (light) cream
½ teaspoon vanilla essence (extract)
2 level teaspoons sifted icing (confectioners') sugar
Grated nutmeg

Pre-heat oven to hot (425°F, Gas Mark 7). Well grease 12 deepish bun tins (muffin cups).

Knead the pastry until smooth then roll out evenly and cut into 12 rounds with a 3 in. biscuit cutter. Use to line the bun tins (muffin cups).

Beat the egg white until just beginning to froth, brush over the inside of the pastry cases then sprinkle with the breadcrumbs (this helps to prevent sogginess).

Beat the whole egg, yolk, cream, essence (extract) and sugar well together, then carefully spoon into the pastry cases. Sprinkle lightly with nutmeg and place just above the centre of the oven.

Reduce the temperature to moderately hot (375°F, Gas Mark 5) and bake for 30–35 minutes or until the custard filling is set and the pastry pale gold.

Leave in the tins (cups) for a few minutes then transfer to a wire (cake) rack. Eat when cold.

Cakes with yeast

Yeast buns and cakes – and all the other bits and pieces that can so easily be produced from a basic dough – are lovely, old-fashioned goodies. But today's busy housewife is luckier than her Grandmother, for research into yeast cooking has made her task easier. For example, rising times can be varied to suit individual circumstances, so in some cases the dough may be made one day and shaped and baked the next. And now a few pointers to success.

Flour
Use plain (all-purpose) flour unless otherwise stated; if the bag says *strong* plain flour as well, so much the better – it gives a lighter textured result.

Yeast
Use fresh yeast if a local baker sells it (blending it with the measured liquid) or dried yeast granules, available in small bags and containers (active dry yeast in aluminium envelopes), if he doesn't.

Fresh yeast is often hard to find, so I usually use dried – 2 level teaspoons (1 envelope) for every

½ oz. fresh (fresh yeast cake) recommended in the recipe. To reconstitute it, just pour some or all of the warm measured liquid into a cup or jug, stir in ½–1 teaspoon sugar and the dried yeast. Leave in a warm place for up to 30 minutes or until the yeast brew froths up.

Rising times
For speed, stand the dough – in its bowl – in a warm place (a sink containing warm to hottish water is ideal) and leave for 30–45 minutes or until the dough has doubled in size.

For a slow rise, leave the dough anywhere in the kitchen for a couple of hours – or less if it doubles up on you!

If tomorrow morning is better for baking than tonight, leave the dough to rise slowly in a larder or pantry (a cool one) for about 12 hours.

If you don't want to bake for 24 hours, leave the dough in the refrigerator (it will rise at a snail's pace), but allow it to reach room temperature before shaping.

To prevent a skin forming on the dough
It should be covered with well greased polythene. If it is to be left in the larder or refrigerator, the dough is best if removed from its bowl and transferred to an oiled polythene bag. If the bag is loosely tied at the top and the bag itself is a reasonable size, there will be adequate room for the dough to expand.

Chelsea buns (left)
Yorkshire tea cakes (right)

Chelsea Buns

Batter ingredients

2 oz. (½ cup) plain (all-purpose) flour
½ level teaspoon sugar
2 level teaspoons (1 envelope) dried yeast
   (active dry yeast)
4 fl. oz. (½ cup) warm milk

Other ingredients

6 oz. (1½ cups) plain (all-purpose) flour
½ level teaspoon salt
Walnut-sized pieces of butter, margarine
   or cooking fat (shortening)
1 standard egg, beaten
Melted butter for brushing
3 oz. (½ cup) dried (chopped) fruit
1 oz. (¼ cup) mixed chopped peel
2 oz. (¼ cup) soft brown sugar
Clear honey for glazing

Blend the batter ingredients together in a large bowl and set aside until frothy, about 20–30 minutes.

Sift together the other flour and salt. Rub in the fat. Mix into the batter ingredients with the beaten egg to give a fairly soft dough that leaves the sides of the bowl clean.

Turn on to a lightly floured surface and knead until smooth and no longer sticky, about 10 minutes. Cover with greased polythene and leave to rise until dough doubles in size. (For rising times, see page 116.)

Turn the risen dough on to a lightly floured surface and flatten with the knuckles to knock out air bubbles. Knead until firm, then roll into a 12 × 9 in. rectangle.

Brush with melted butter and sprinkle with the fruit, peel and sugar.

Roll up from the longest side, like a Swiss roll (jelly roll), and seal the edge. Cut into 9 equal slices and place, cut side down, in a lightly greased 7 in. square cake tin (pan) or small roasting tin (baking pan). Cover with polythene and leave to rise at room temperature for about 30 minutes or until the dough feels springy.

Remove the polythene and bake near the top of a moderately hot oven (375°F, Gas Mark 5) for 30–35 minutes. Lift out of the tin (pan), transfer to a wire (cake) rack and brush with clear honey.

Yorkshire Tea Cakes

1 level teaspoon sugar
½ pint (1¼ cups) lukewarm milk
2 level teaspoons (1 envelope) dried yeast
   (active dry yeast)
1 lb. (4 cups) plain (all-purpose) flour
1 level teaspoon salt
1 oz. (2 T) lard or white cooking fat
   (shortening)
2 level tablespoons (2½ T) castor
   (granulated) sugar
4 level tablespoons (5 T) currants

Hot cross buns 1 : Frothy yeast liquid being added to dry ingredients

2 : Mixture being kneaded to a dough

3 : Kneading dough into a ball; buns, with cross cut, placed on baking tray (cookie sheet)

Hot cross buns (behind right) and lardy cake (left)

Dissolve a teaspoon sugar in warm milk then sprinkle yeast on top. Leave in warm place for 20–30 minutes or until frothy.

Sift the flour and salt into a bowl. Rub in the fat. Add the sugar and currants and toss lightly together.

Mix to a dough with the yeast liquid. Knead thoroughly until the dough is smooth, elastic and no longer sticky, 15–20 minutes. Return to the bowl, cover with greased polythene and leave to rise until double in size. (For rising times, see page 116.)

Turn out on to a floured surface and divide into 6 equal pieces. Knead each piece lightly into a 6 in. round. Transfer to 2 large, well greased baking trays (sheets), cover with greased polythene and leave to rise in warm place until light and puffy, 30–40 minutes.

Uncover and bake just above the centre of a moderately hot oven (400°F, Gas Mark 6) for 20 minutes. Cool on a wire (cake) rack.

Before serving, split open, toast if liked and thickly spread with butter.

Hot Cross Buns

Make as for Bath Buns (p. 120), sifting the flour with 1 level teaspoon mixed spice and ½ level teaspoon *each* cinnamon and nutmeg. Substitute mixed (chopped) dried fruit for sultanas (raisins) but include the same amount of peel. When the dough has risen, knead quickly until smooth and divide into 12 equal pieces. Knead each into a ball and transfer to a well greased baking tray (sheet). Cover with polythene and leave to rise in a warm place until almost double in size.

Cut a cross on top of each then bake just above the centre of a hot oven (425°F, Gas Mark 7) for 20–25 minutes. Remove from the oven and glaze by brushing with honey or melted apricot jam (preserves). Cool on a wire (cake) rack.

Lardy Cake

½ teaspoon sugar
½ pint (1¼ cups) lukewarm water
2 level teaspoons (1 envelope) dried yeast (active dry yeast)
1 lb. (4 cups) plain (all-purpose) flour
2 level teaspoons salt
4 oz. (½ cup) lard or cooking fat (shortening)
4 level tablespoons (5 T) castor (granulated) sugar
1 level teaspoon mixed spice

Dissolve ½ teaspoon sugar in some of the warm water. Sprinkle the yeast on top. Leave in a warm place for about 20–30 minutes or until frothy.

Sift the flour and salt into a bowl. Work to a dough with the yeast liquid and remaining water.

Knead for about 20 minutes or until the dough is smooth and elastic and no longer sticky. Cover with greased polythene and leave to rise until double in size. (For rising times, see page 116.)

Turn the dough on to a floured surface and roll out into a large oblong. Working from the top end, cover two-thirds of the dough with flakes of fat, using half the amount. Sprinkle with 2 tablespoons sugar and ½ teaspoon spice. Dredge lightly with flour. Fold up by bringing the bottom third over the centre and the top third over that. Seal the edges with a rolling pin then turn the dough round so that the folds are to the right and left.

Roll out again into an oblong and cover with remaining flakes of fat, sugar and spice as before. Fold into 3 as before and seal edges with a rolling pin. Turn the dough so that the folded edges are again to the left and right, then roll into an oval ½ in. thick.

Transfer to a greased baking tray (sheet) and cover with greased polythene. Leave to rise in a warm place until light and puffy, 20–30 minutes. Uncover and bake near the top of a hot oven (425°F, Gas Mark 7) for about 30 minutes. Serve hot with butter.

Bath Buns

½ level teaspoon sugar
5 tablespoons (6¼ T) lukewarm water
5 level teaspoons (2 envelopes) dried yeast (active dry yeast)
1 lb. (4 cups) plain (all-purpose) flour
1 level teaspoon salt
2 oz. (¼ cup) butter or margarine
2 level tablespoons (2½ T) castor (granulated) sugar
4 oz. (1 cup) sultanas (golden raisins)
2 oz. (⅓ cup) mixed chopped peel
¼ pint (⅝ cup) lukewarm milk
1 large egg
Beaten egg for brushing
About 8 cubes of sugar, coarsely crushed

Dissolve ½ teaspoon sugar in water and sprinkle the yeast on top. Leave in a warm place for 20–30 minutes or until frothy.

Sift the flour and salt into a bowl. Rub in the fat finely then add the sugar, sultanas (golden raisins) and peel. Mix to a soft dough with the yeast liquid and the milk, beaten with the egg.

Turn on to a floured surface and knead until the dough is smooth and elastic and no longer sticky, 15–20 minutes. Cover with greased polythene and leave to rise until double in size. (For rising times see page 116.)

Turn on to a floured surface and knead lightly.

English muffins

Put 12–14 tablespoons dough (shape should be irregular) on to a large greased baking tray (sheet) and cover with greased polythene. Leave to rise in a warm place for about 30 minutes or until almost double in size.

Uncover, brush with egg and sprinkle with crushed sugar. Bake just above the centre of a hot oven (425°F, Gas Mark 7) for 20–25 minutes. Cool on a wire (cake) rack.

English Muffins

½ teaspoon sugar
6 tablespoons (7½ T) lukewarm water
4 level teaspoons (2 envelopes) dried yeast (active dry yeast)
1 lb. (4 cups) plain (all-purpose) flour
1 level teaspoon salt
¼ pint (⅝ cup) lukewarm milk

1 standard egg, beaten
1 oz. (2 T) butter, melted

Dissolve ½ teaspoon sugar in warm water.
Sprinkle the yeast on top and leave in a warm
place for 20–30 minutes or until frothy.

Sift the flour and salt into a bowl and mix to a
softish dough with the yeast liquid, milk, egg
and butter.

Turn on to a well floured surface and knead
until the dough is smooth and elastic and no
longer sticky, about 20 minutes. Cover with
greased polythene and leave to rise until double
in size. (For rising times, see page 116.)

Turn on to a floured board, knead lightly and
roll out to ½ in. thickness. Cut into 12 rounds
with a 3½ in. plain biscuit cutter, using up trimmings. Grease 2 large baking trays (sheets) and
dust with flour. Put 6 muffins on to each and

dust with more flour. Cover and leave to rise
until dough doubles in size.

Uncover and bake towards the top of a very hot
oven (450°F, Gas Mark 8) for 5 minutes. Turn
the muffins over and bake for a further 5–6
minutes. To serve, toast on both sides, pull
apart, butter thickly and put together again.

Spiced Almond Ring

½ teaspoon sugar
¼ pint less 3 tablespoons (½ cup less 1 T)
  lukewarm milk
2 level teaspoons (1 envelope) dried yeast
  (active dry yeast)
8 oz. (2 cups) plain (all-purpose) flour
½ level teaspoon salt
Walnut-sized piece of butter, melted
1 standard egg, beaten

Filling and decoration

1 walnut-sized piece of butter, melted
2 oz. ($\frac{1}{4}$ cup) soft brown sugar
1 level teaspoon ground allspice
1 oz. ($\frac{1}{4}$ cup) almonds, blanched and chopped
2 oz. (just under $\frac{1}{2}$ cup) icing (confectioners') sugar, sifted
1$\frac{1}{2}$ teaspoons warm water
4 glacé cherries, halved
1 tablespoon (1$\frac{1}{4}$ T) flaked almonds

Dissolve $\frac{1}{2}$ teaspoon sugar in warm milk then sprinkle yeast on top. Leave in a warm place for 20–30 minutes or until frothy.

Sift the flour and salt into a bowl, then mix to a dough with the yeast liquid, butter and egg.

Knead on a lightly floured surface for about 10–15 minutes until smooth, elastic and no longer sticky. Cover with greased polythene and leave to rise until double in size. (For rising times, see page 116.)

Uncover and roll into a 12 × 9 in. rectangle. Brush with melted butter then sprinkle with the sugar, spice and almonds.

Roll up as for a Swiss roll (jelly roll), starting from one of the longer sides, and seal the edges. Bring the roll ends together to form a ring, seal by pinching together and put on to a greased baking tray (sheet).

With scissors, cut at 1 in. intervals to within $\frac{1}{2}$ in. of the centre and separate by turning each piece gently sideways. Cover with greased polythene

and leave to rise in a warm place for about 30 minutes. Uncover then bake near the top of a moderately hot oven (375°F, Gas Mark 5) for 30–35 minutes. Cool on a wire (cake) rack.

To decorate: make glacé icing from the icing (confectioners') sugar and water. Pour over the ring and decorate with cherries and flaked almonds.

Christmas Garland

2 level teaspoons (1 envelope) dried yeast (active dry yeast)
4 tablespoons (5 T) lukewarm water
4 tablespoons (5 T) lukewarm milk
1 level tablespoon (1 T) castor (granulated) sugar
3 tablespoons (3$\frac{3}{4}$ T) corn oil
1 egg yolk
8 oz. (2 cups) plain (all-purpose) flour
1 level teaspoon salt

Filling

4 oz. ($\frac{1}{2}$ cup) butter
4 oz. ($\frac{1}{2}$ cup) soft brown sugar
1 tablespoon rum
2 oz. (just under $\frac{1}{2}$ cup) sultanas (golden raisins)
1 tablespoon (1$\frac{1}{4}$ T) mixed chopped peel
1 tablespoon (1$\frac{1}{4}$ T) currants
1 tablespoon (1$\frac{1}{4}$ T) chopped angelica
2 oz. (just under $\frac{1}{2}$ cup) seedless raisins
2 tablespoons glacé cherries, chopped

Spiced almond ring

Dissolve the yeast in the lukewarm water.

Mix together the milk, sugar, oil and egg yolk.

Sift the flour and salt into a bowl then work to a dough with the yeast and the oil mixture.

Knead until the dough is smooth, elastic and no longer sticky, about 15 minutes. Cover with greased polythene and leave to rise until double in size. (For rising times, see page 116.)

Roll the dough into an oblong about 24 × 6 in.

Combine all the filling ingredients and spread on the dough, leaving a 1 in. margin uncovered all the way round.

Moisten the edges with water and roll up from the longer side like a Swiss roll (jelly roll). Form the roll into a ring shape, joining the ends, then transfer to a well greased baking tray (sheet). Slit the top of the dough at intervals with sharp knife, then cover with greased polythene and leave to rise in a warm place until double in size, about 30 minutes.

Uncover and bake just above the centre of a hot oven (425°F, Gas Mark 7) for 20–25 minutes.

When cold, ice the ring with glacé icing: sift 6 oz. (just over 1 cup) icing (confectioners') sugar and mix to a smooth icing with a few teaspoons orange juice. Pour over the garland and when set, decorate with preserved fruit.

Bara Brith

Bara Brith or Fruited Welsh Bread

1 teaspoon sugar

$\frac{1}{4}$ pint + 2 tablespoons ($\frac{3}{4}$ cup) lukewarm water

1 level tablespoon (2 envelopes) dried yeast (active dry yeast)

1 lb. (4 cups) plain (all-purpose) flour

1 level teaspoon *each* mixed spice and salt

3 oz. (4 T) margarine or cooking fat (shortening)

3 oz. (6 T) soft brown sugar

1$\frac{1}{2}$ lb. (just under 5 cups) mixed dried (chopped) fruit

1 large egg, beaten

Well grease two 1 lb. loaf tins (2 cup capacity oblong loaf pans). Dissolve teaspoon sugar in warm water then sprinkle the yeast on top. Leave in warm place 20–30 minutes or until frothy.

Sift the flour, spice and salt into a bowl. Rub in the fat finely then add the sugar and fruit. Mix to a dough with the yeast liquid and egg.

Knead for a good 20 minutes or until the dough is smooth, elastic and no longer sticky. Cover with greased polythene and leave to rise until double in size. (For rising times, see page 116.)

Turn on to a floured board and knead

thoroughly. Divide in 2 and shape to fit the prepared tins (pans). Stand both on a baking tray (cookie sheet), cover with greased polythene and leave in warm place to rise until the dough reaches the tops of the tins (pans).

Uncover and bake in the centre of a moderate oven (350°F, Gas Mark 4) for 50–60 minutes. Leave in the tins (pans) for 5 minutes then turn out on to a wire (cake) rack.

If liked, glaze by brushing with clear honey. Leave until completely cold before cutting.

Danish-style Christmas Cake

$\frac{1}{2}$ teaspoon sugar

$\frac{1}{4}$ pint ($\frac{5}{8}$ cup) lukewarm milk

4 level teaspoons (2 envelopes) dried yeast (active dry yeast)

1 lb. (4 cups) plain (all-purpose) flour

$\frac{1}{2}$ level teaspoon salt

1 level teaspoon cinnamon

$\frac{1}{2}$ level teaspoon mixed spice

2 level tablespoons (2$\frac{1}{2}$ T) castor (granulated) sugar

8 oz. (1$\frac{1}{2}$ cups) mixed (chopped) dried fruit

4 oz. ($\frac{1}{2}$ cup) Danish (sweet) butter, melted

2 standard eggs, beaten

About 1 dozen cubes of sugar, crushed

4 level tablespoons flaked almonds

Well grease a 7 × 11 in. cake tin (pan) or roasting tin (baking pan) and line the base and sides with greased greaseproof (waxed) paper.

Dissolve $\frac{1}{2}$ teaspoon of sugar in milk, sprinkle the yeast on top. Leave in a warm place for 20–30 minutes or until frothy.

Sift the flour, salt, cinnamon and spice into bowl. Add the sugar and fruit. Mix to a dough with the yeast liquid, three-quarters of the butter and the beaten eggs.

Using the hand, beat in the bowl until the dough is firm, then knead thoroughly until it is smooth,

elastic and no longer sticky, about 20 minutes. Transfer to the prepared tin (pan). Cover and leave to rise until the dough reaches the top of the tin (pan). (For rising times, see page 116.)
Brush the top with remaining butter then sprinkle with the crushed sugar and almonds.
Bake in the centre of a moderately hot oven (400°F, Gas Mark 6) for 30 minutes or until well risen and firm. Leave in the tin (pan) for 5 minutes then turn out and cool on a wire (cake) rack.
Serve freshly baked. Any left-over cake should be stored in an air-tight container and then served sliced and buttered.

Traditional Doughnuts

$\frac{1}{2}$ teaspoon sugar
6 tablespoons ($7\frac{1}{2}$ T) lukewarm milk
2 level teaspoons (1 envelope) dried yeast (active dry yeast)
8 oz. (2 cups) plain (all-purpose) flour
$\frac{1}{2}$ level teaspoon salt
Walnut-sized piece of butter or margarine
1 standard egg, beaten
Jam (preserves) for filling
2 oz. ($\frac{1}{4}$ cup) castor (granulated) sugar
$\frac{1}{2}$ level teaspoon cinnamon

Dissolve sugar in milk then sprinkle the yeast on top. Leave in a warm place for 20–30 minutes or until frothy.
Sift the flour and salt into a bowl. Rub in the fat finely, then mix to a soft dough with the yeast liquid and egg.
Turn on to a lightly floured surface and knead until smooth and no longer sticky, about 10 minutes. Cover with greased polythene and leave to rise until double in size. (For rising times, see page 116.)
Turn on to a floured surface and knead thoroughly. Divide into 12 equal pieces and roll each into a ball. Make a deep depression with the handle of a wooden spoon in each, fill with a little jam then pinch up the edges of the dough around the jam so that it is completely enclosed. Cover with greased polythene and leave in a warm place to rise until double in size.
Uncover and deep fry in hot (but not smoking) oil for approximately 4 minutes. Drain thoroughly and roll in sugar and cinnamon.

Doughnut Rings

Divide the risen dough into 12 pieces and shape each into longish rolls. Join the ends together to form rings. Cover with polythene and leave in a warm place to rise until double in size. Fry and finish as Traditional Doughnuts (above).

Doughnut Splits

Divide the risen dough into 12 pieces and shape into 4 in. long ovals. Cover with oiled polythene and leave in a warm place to rise until double in size. Fry and drain as Traditional Doughnuts (above). If liked, toss in castor (granulated) sugar. When cold, split in half lengthwise and fill with jam (preserves) and whipped cream.

All-Bran Tea-Bread

1 teaspoon sugar
$\frac{1}{4}$ pint ($\frac{5}{8}$ cup) lukewarm water
1 level tablespoon (1 envelope) dried yeast (active dry yeast)
3 oz. (about $1\frac{1}{2}$ cups) all-bran
$\frac{1}{4}$ pint ($\frac{5}{8}$ cup) milk
1 lb. (4 cups) plain (all-purpose) flour
1 level teaspoon salt
1 oz. ($\frac{1}{8}$ cup) sugar
Grated peel of $\frac{1}{2}$ orange
1 standard egg, beaten
4 oz. (1 cup) icing (confectioners') sugar, sifted
Little hot water
Chopped glacé cherries, glacé pineapple and angelica

Dissolve 1 teaspoon sugar in warm water and sprinkle the yeast on top.
Leave for 20 minutes or until frothy.
Put the all-bran and milk into a bowl and leave for 10 minutes. Sift the flour and salt into the same basin. Add the sugar, orange peel, egg and yeast. Add liquid and knead to a soft dough. Continue kneading until the dough is smooth and elastic and no longer sticky, about 20 minutes. Cover with greased polythene and leave to rise until double in size. (For rising times, see page 116.)
Turn onto a floured board and knead lightly for 1–2 minutes. Divide into 3 and roll into ropes about 15 in. long. Make into a plait then join the two ends together to make a ring. Stand on a greased baking tray (sheet), cover with greased polythene and leave in a warm place to rise for about 15 minutes until double in size.
Uncover and bake towards the top of a hot oven (425°F, Gas Mark 7) for about 15–20 minutes. Cool on a wire (cake) rack.
Mix the icing (confectioners') sugar with a little hot water to give a coating consistency and trickle over the tea-bread. Sprinkle with glacé fruits when the icing has almost set.

Index

Acknowledgments

The following colour photographs are by courtesy of:
Cadbury Schweppes: p. 6; 40 (above); 48 (below); 66; 71 (above right); 100 (below); 105 (below)   Conway Picture Library: p. 36 (above); 41 (above); 100 (above left)   Danish Centre: p. 71 (above left); 112 (above right)   Kellogs Kitchen: p. 112 (below)   Mazola: p. 100 (above right); 97 (above); 112 (above left)   PAF International: p. 11; 14; 33 (below left); 40–41; 44; 67 (above); 70; 71 (below); 74–75; 78; 79; 104; 105 (above)   RHM Foods: p. 36 (below)   Syndication International: p. 33 (above); 33 (below right); 37; 48 (above); 97 (below); 108–9
The following black and white pictures are by courtesy of:
Australian Recipe Service: p. 68   Blue Band: p. 8; 27; 34; 83; 90–91; 92; 98; 110; 111   Blue Ribbon Spices: p. 62–63   British Sugar Bureau: p. 1; 53; 54–55   Butter Information Council: p. 39 (below right)   Cadbury Schweppes: p. 42 (below right); 49; 52   Canned and Packaged Foods Bureau: p. 80   Flour Advisory Bureau: p. 13; 16; 18–19; 20; 24–25; 28; 29; 31; 32; 35; 38; 39; 42 (above left); 43; 51; 56; 58; 59; 61; 65; 76 (above left); 85; 86–7; 94–5; 96; 106–7; 109; 113 (below); 114 (below); 115; 117; 118; 119; 120–121; 122; 123; 125   Kellog's: p. 17; 81; 89   Kraft Foods Limited: p. 22–23; 45   Mazola: p. 50; 114 (above)   National Dairy Council: p. 46; 76 (below right)   Princes Malayan Pineapple: p. 113 (above)   Stork: p. 116

1:5